The First Rule
of Selling

How StorageMart Led
an Industry
Out of Recession

Tron Jordheim

The First Rule of Selling: How StorageMart Led an Industry out of Recession

Published by Wheatmark®
1760 East River Road, Suite 145
Tucson, Arizona 85718 USA
www.wheatmark.com

ISBN: 978-1-62787-027-6 (paperback)
ISBN: 978-1-62787-028-3 (ebook)
LCCN: 2013942865

rev201301

Contents

Introduction
Your Sales Culture Could
Be a Lot Better

StorageMart represents only a tiny fraction of the self storage business in North America. Some estimates say there are about 50,000 self storage facilities between the United States and Canada. That means StorageMart's 135 properties represent only .0027 of the entire storage business. How is it that a company with such a small piece of the pie had enough influence to lead an entire industry out of the last recession? The storage business is primarily made up of single facility owners, regional players, and a few larger operators. With 135 properties, StorageMart is one of the largest privately held storage companies in the world. That distinction makes other people in the industry take notice. When StorageMart starts to make moves, others pay attention. This is the story of how it came to be that one company helped lead an entire industry out of recession.

The first assertion I want you to take from this book is: *Your sales culture could be a lot better*.

If you compared your business to the self storage business, you might be embarrassed to see how well many storage operators have embraced a sales culture.

Since you picked up this book, you are curious about creating, improving, or retooling the approach you and your company take in your sales and customer service activities. You have a thirst for the knowledge of sales, or the title of the book would not have piqued your interest. Why else would you want to know more? Are you curious about one of the most interesting phenomena of modern times, the self-storage industry? Perhaps your curiosity is in learning about the companies that thrived during and after the economic upheaval of 2007 to 2012. In any case, I hope you find the next few hours well spent.

I am betting you probably agree that even good companies could find a percentage or two of revenue and profit enhancement from doing a better job of doing more business with new clients and customers. If so, you and I are already on the same page.

So let's focus on my first assertion: *Your sales culture could be a lot better.* Why did I choose this particular assertion and phrase it the way I did? After all, I could have chosen a more challenging assertion such as *Do you really think your company's sales culture is any good?* Or I could have picked a brusque attention-getter such as *Hey, your company's sales culture sucks!* I could have picked something more academic-sounding such as *Stimulating a 12 percent improvement in bottom line corporate profits through the institution of sales culture enhancements.* I could have even used a boastful approach: *I quintupled the revenue of my company by creating a sales culture . . . and so could you!*

Any one of these might express my feelings about the value of a good sales culture and my opinion of most companies' current sales and customer service practices, but as someone who claims to be a sales culture practitioner, I thought I'd better start off by *acting* like someone who practices a good sales culture. Let me explain.

I didn't want to challenge you because, if you read this assertion, *Do you really think your company's sales culture is any good?* while browsing through a book at a bookstore or while perusing a website, you might just answer the question to yourself, *Yeah, it's good enough for now* and forget all about reading my book. You might also think I was taking a snippy tone, in which case you probably wouldn't want to read any further.

If I picked the brusque-worded assertion, accusing you and your company of having a lousy sales culture, you might become defensive and shut me out. Perhaps even worse, you might associate my book and me with any number of obnoxious know-it-alls you have to deal with on a regular basis, and I would never have you for a customer, client, acquaintance, fan, or friend. Not ever.

Likewise, the academic assertion would probably discourage you from even reading the entire phrase before thinking *boring!* and walking away. If you read the whole phrase, you might think, *That is an admirable goal: 12 percent revenue growth, but I wasn't planning on napping right now, so an academic treatise is about the last thing I need to read.*

And the boastful assertion? Like most people who are proud of their accomplishments, I'd love to boast about one success or another. But if you are like most people, you really hate it when people start the first conversation they have with you by boasting about one thing or another. I'd rather you didn't roll your eyes at my book and walk away.

Instead, I want to start a conversation with you. That's why I chose to phrase my first assertion as *Your sales culture could be a lot better.* Because I'm pretty certain that it could. More than likely, this is a suggestion that can lead to a productive dialogue. After all, there is always room for improvement.

I went with this particular assertion because I believe in practicing what I preach. This assertion reflects the approach a good sales culture needs to take. A good sales culture acknowledges that people are always having an internal dialogue with themselves. One goal of a sales culture is to bring its particular topic into the internal dialogues of its audience. I hope to get you talking to yourself about how you feel about the sales culture (or lack of sales culture) in your workplace. One great way to help people start talking to themselves about your favorite topic is to make a legitimate and relevant suggestion.

I could have tried another approach that is common in a sales culture. I could have asked you a qualifying or open-ended question: "So, how do you think your sales culture is doing?" I also could have asked an alternate-choice question: "Is your sales culture thriving, or do you feel it might need some nurturing?"

I didn't choose either because I only have one shot at becoming the subject of your internal dialogue. If I asked a qualifying question, you might answer that question in your own mind without thinking any more about my premise.

I did not see a chance to get in a follow-up question, so I thought I'd better go with the suggestion. I was afraid you would put my qualifying question out of your mind in a split second and then become distracted by another book you might see near mine, such as the latest book by a pundit or politician such as the one I saw the other day: "I am a sociopathic megalomaniac, and I don't care how many people I hurt stroking my own abundant ego."

So instead I chose to go with a suggestion, a suggestion that you will likely answer yes to... and then think about. No matter what your role at work is, and no matter what your career path looks like, I am pretty sure the corporate culture you live in could benefit from an increased emphasis on selling. Unless you walk around in a haze every day, you have probably had the same thought yourself.

After putting all that careful thought into coming up with a lead-off assertion for this section, I decided to put you on the spot. If people in the self-storage business are working hard to develop a good sales culture, do you have an excuse for not working hard on your own sales culture? There are not a lot of businesses as dull as renting storage units to people. There is no glamour. There is nothing interesting going on. Yet it is a business that has made great strides by adopting a sales culture. Maybe your business is as dull as renting storage units. Maybe it is exciting and fun. Either way, you could benefit from revisiting the sales culture concept and building or rebuilding one in your business.

Your business is surely going through challenges. Adopting a sales culture was how the self-storage business managed to not crash and burn during the big downturn. Perhaps the time is right for you to lead a sales culture adoption now.

So how can I help you improve your personal sales culture and the sales culture of your company? I am going to give you the four steps we took at StorageMart to boost our business. I am going to frame these four steps for you in such a way that you can make an effective and immediate impact whether you are a frontline worker, supervisor, unit manager, or CEO.

Everyone in all positions at all levels can push the adoption of sales culture improvements. The least you will gain from reading this book is to see personal improvement in your daily business interactions and better performance figures for the areas for which you are personally responsible. This may just be for you to use for yourself to further your career or to give you more knowledge, insight, and ability.

You can also use the four steps to make deep improvements to your entire business unit or your whole company. The idea of having a sales culture is not new. But the promise of improving what you have is huge.

Whether you are buying a single copy of this book to gain a personal edge in your job or career, or whether you are planning on getting it into the hands of everyone up and down your organizational chart, take time to let your internal dialogue flow. Discuss with yourself how these four ways to boost your company's sales culture can be put into practice in small and big ways.

Some of what you see here is a part of the sales and marketing guide, *Rent it Up*, which I put out to the self-storage business in 2009 to highlight some practices that worked well for us.

What does any of this have to do with the first rule of selling? A rule doesn't make sense unless you have a context within which to apply the rule. Keep reading as I build the context.

Lead by Living a Sales Culture

Why do we want to live a sales culture? What's the point? It's a lot of work. It's a lot of trouble. If you are not currently living a sales culture, integrating it into your practices and approaches is going to throw your current operations into a certain amount of chaos. You can't just say, "And now we have a sales culture" and expect everything to fall into place. Each person in your group, team, or company has their own notions of what that might mean, and probably no two of them match. Until you get everyone on the same page and until you build systems and practices that allow people to find the page and get on it, you are going to have a mess on your hands.

Living a sales culture requires good leadership and management skills from you and your staff. Some of your favorite employees are going to have a hard time adjusting. You're going to end up firing a few people you like because they won't fit into a new cultural system. You're going to have a hard time finding people to hire as new employees who have what it takes to thrive in a sales culture. You are going to have a hard time figuring out how to hire people who fit into a sales culture. Why do you think businesses look to software, automation, and customer self-service to solve business problems? Sure, these approaches are great for driving down the cost of certain functions and processes. But the biggest reason is the unpredictable and inconsistent performance of people. The fewer people involved, the less chance of things going haywire. People need constant monitoring, coaching, and training to perform tasks. Even rote process tasks need lots of supervision. A great sales culture may have routines, practices, established rituals, and ethics, but it is in constant development. Not all of the people you think will live up to a sales culture will work out for you. You will require a special kind of person. You are going to become that special kind of person. You are going to devote time, emotion, energy, money, and effort. So what's the point?

Since you are interested in the subject, chances are you agree that it's better to have a sales-savvy staff than to not have a sales-savvy staff. Correct? Okay, great! That is a good jumping-off point. Call it strategy; call it philosophy; call it keeping up with your competition. If you believe you should have a sales culture, then it will be worth creating a sales culture. But are you sure you want to go through the trouble?

A school of thought says: "Don't worry about it. If you have a decent offering, your prices are okay, you have a good conversion funnel on your website, and you do a lot of advertising, then it doesn't matter. As long as people can find you when they need your offering, you can do business with enough of them, and you don't have to have very good salespeople." Do you subscribe to that theory? If you do, you may be looking at the wrong book. You should be looking at *Good Enough . . . Five Easy Ways to Make a Profit Without Putting Out Much Effort, Time, or Money*.

Perhaps it is not such a bad strategy, the *good enough* strategy. It is a lot less trouble and a lot less expensive. You will invest a lot less sweat and energy. If you are happy getting a little cash flow without running a very good business, or without building much long-term value into your brands and assets, then go for it. Be just *good enough*.

If you are trying to create as much profit as you can and build a sustainable business as well as assets that will increase in value far faster than your competitors' assets, then you are in the right place, and you should keep reading.

Initiatives, changes, and efforts are supposed to be all about the results they bring. What are the organizational results of creating and living a sales culture? There are three results in store for you: selling to more people, keeping current customers longer, and generating more revenue per customer. If you could sell to two or three more people a month than you do now, if your company could sell to two or three more people a month at each location, in each product category, at each distribution point, what would the added value be to you? Whatever value your average customer offers you, it's worth getting more customers, right? No matter what sort of a market you are in, there's a lot of money involved, isn't there?

Let me ask you this: are you getting a significant amount of your new business from referrals? Do you think you're getting up to 20 percent of your new business from referrals? Are you getting more than 20 percent? Let's go with 20 percent. If that is the case, the added value of the new customer has even more impact; if you get five new ones, you will have an additional new one from a referral. So you are buying six customers for the price of five. That's one heck of a deal!

In businesses that are not focused on a sales culture, that number might be significantly lower. They may be buying eleven customers for the price of ten or twenty-one customers for the price of twenty. That doesn't sound nearly as good. This is just one reason why creating a sales culture is so important.

Another part of the puzzle is keeping customers longer. It doesn't do you any good if you bring in more people but even more people leave as customers. So what would the added value be to you if your customer stayed for an additional transaction or two or three? It would be tremendous.

An increase of two transactions in the life cycle of your customer is significant whether you are selling pizza or jet planes.

If your sales culture is working, you're also cross-selling and up-selling with better proficiency, moving more goods and services out the door. This might mean your $1,000 customer is now a $1,100 customer. It just keeps getting better.

The ultimate result of your sales culture is a significant rise in the value of your assets. The value of your business is its revenue times whatever the capitalization rate is for your industry. It is not unusual in many industries, especially those involving real estate assets, for the market value to be ten times the revenue. If this is true, then every dollar you create translates into ten dollars in value. This ought to be enough motivation to make you a passionate sales culture maniac.

It sounds easy enough, doesn't it? On the one hand it is simple. The whole customer experience can be boiled down to pain-and-plea-sure stimulus—the behavior of customers continues to be strongly influenced by basic instinct: avoid pain and seek pleasure.

Is it a pain to do business with you, or do you make it easy for people? Is it a pleasure to be your customer? Is it a pain to end a business relationship with you? Or do people quit your company because it is a pain to be a customer? Managing the pains and plea-sures people associate with your business lays the foundation work for creating your sales culture.

I got my start in the sales culture in the sixth grade. Many of my friends had jobs. Most of the kids my age were sacking or delivering groceries, and I thought those guys worked awfully hard for very little money. I noticed glass windows everywhere along the retail streets where I lived in Brooklyn, New York. Only the adults were washing those windows, using buckets, squeegees, and ladders. But most of the glass I could reach without a ladder, and one could buy window cleaner in a spray can. So I got myself a roll of paper towels and a can of window cleaner and started a window-cleaning busi-ness. I stopped in on all the retail businesses and offices that lined the main shopping street in my neighborhood and created an office win-dow-cleaning route for myself. The small business owners thought it was cute to let an ambitious kid have the business, especially since I was a lot more affordable than using an established cleaning busi-ness. I was making three times what my buddies were making deliv-ering groceries, and I thought, *You know, this entrepreneur life isn't bad*, and I've been at it ever since. I've started companies from nothing and turned them into something. I managed salespeople, ran mar-keting programs, created business models, and sent lots of dollars to the bottom line.

I showed how one creates a sales culture by helping to create the PhoneSmart Off-Site Sales Force. PhoneSmart was founded by Stor-ageMart, one of North America's largest self-storage providers, to serve as a call center in order to turn missed phone calls at self-stor-age properties into rental opportunities. PhoneSmart was created not just to help StorageMart grow its business, but to serve other storage owners who were looking for ways to improve their businesses. We created selling systems, training systems, sales auditing systems, and new ways to generate customers. This helped us to learn how self-storage customers think and act and how owners and managers of self-storage properties think and act. PhoneSmart celebrated its twelfth anniversary in 2012 and has served storage properties in the United States, Canada, and Latin America. In PhoneSmart's first twelve years, its sales agents had more than three million conversations with self-storage tenants and prospective customers. We sent our clients more than one million leads and reservations. We continue to tweak our systems and create new service offerings that help our clients rent to more people, keep them longer, and generate more revenue from each customer. Our business thrives by constantly raising the sales culture bar, and because we regularly refresh and reinvent that culture.

The point of this paragraph is to tell you that I have real world, successful, day-to-day knowledge to pass on to you. I also share this with you to give you a hint as to how one can create a sales culture in a larger company. The PhoneSmart parent company, StorageMart, was not founded as a sales organization, but as a real estate holding company. PhoneSmart became its sales culture laboratory. When the influences and effects of the PhoneSmart sales culture on StorageMart became apparent, the next logical step was to spread that culture to all of StorageMart.

You might not be impressed at first by sales and management advice coming from someone who currently works in the self-storage business. Do some research to find out which real estate sector fared the best during the difficult times of 2007 through 2012. The answer is self-storage, a business that did far better than other businesses in this recession because self-storage operators felt their market overheating before other real estate businesses did. They saw overbuilding and market saturation in many parts of the country. They felt the land-value bubble inflating. They felt the cost of construction materials and labor push higher and higher. New developments started looking risky in 2005, and by 2006 storage operators had cut way back on new projects. The major players intentionally stopped the self-storage building boom that took place from 2000 through 2005 because deals no longer penciled out.

Self-storage also turned out to be the best-performing real estate sector during that recession, a recession that devastated some real estate sectors, because self-storage has short-term leases on small spaces. Every tenant is a month-to-month tenant, and the average space is a hundred square feet. When commercial and office tenants started leaving their landlords, it became difficult to replace them. When tenants began to return to office and commercial projects in 2010 and 2011, they negotiated incredible bargains that will last at least three to five years. Self-storage was not put in that situation.

The main reason many self-storage businesses fared so well in comparison with other businesses was because self-storage was undergoing a cultural shift at the same time as the economy was about to crash.

Self-storage has always been a real estate management play where all you need is a good, clean location and the ability to collect the rent. There has been enough demand from the inception of the industry in the 1960s through about 2002 in most markets, and supply remained low enough that new projects filled themselves up.

As the market began to get crowded, consumers began to get educated. Competition heated up with the rise of the Internet, where people could easily research storage places in their areas.

In a moment in business where competition is hot, potential customers are not easily swayed, and expenses are rising, there is only one reasonable response, which is to turn into a sales-and-marketing-driven business. It took a while to make this happen, but one by one, the storage operators got smarter about marketing their businesses. In order to obtain a profitable and attractive return on those marketing dollars, storage companies started learning to sell.

StorageMart and PhoneSmart were among the few leading the way. Like many industries, self-storage has trade shows where vendors such as PhoneSmart can pitch their offerings to owners and operators. In 2002, storage trade show attendees would stop at the PhoneSmart booth and ask, "Why on Earth would I need a call center?" The PhoneSmart people explained that most self-storage properties miss about fifty or sixty phone calls a month because those calls come in when the facility is closed or during business hours when the staff is busy doing other things. Those fifty phone calls boiled down to twenty new storage rental inquiries, from which PhoneSmart salespeople created sixteen leads and reservations of which six or eight would rent. Those six or eight new rentals had a lifetime value of $500 to $1,000 depending on the market.

Most people who already had some sort of a sales culture in place would have heard all of that and made a few quick calculations. They might have said, "Let's see, I can get $3,000 to $8,000 gross revenue, which my bankers would see as a $30,000 to $80,000 increase in my real estate asset value, each month for about $400 a month. What the heck am I waiting for? Sign me up!" But that was not the typical response for many years. Most people were not interested in spending the money or going through the hassle of following up on the leads and reservations.

As of 2013, trade show attendees no longer ask why they should use a call center for their storage properties. They now know clearly why they should. Their question is now, "Why should I use PhoneSmart?" This interesting shift came about because people saw what happened to businesses that had a sales culture in place. These businesses survived well during the worst days of 2008 and 2009 and then thrived from 2010 through 2013.

Self-storage experienced an interesting confluence of factors from 2007 through 2009 that forced sales cultures to grow quickly. On the one hand, it began to get more difficult to fill empty space, as current tenants were moving out faster than new tenants were moving in. The economic crash wiped out many small businesses and most of the contractors who were dependent on the building trades. Many of these businesses used self-storage. The abrupt halt to the housing market took away a big chunk of new tenants as well. Many storage places did a lot of business from people moving into new subdivisions, people buying up and people moving from old homes to new, first-time home buyers, and people cashing in on the enormous equity some older Americans held. At the same time, self-storage operators began closing a higher percentage of their rental inquiries and driving more rental inquires by stepping up their sales and marketing games.

You might think that self-storage benefited from the foreclosure catastrophe and the downsizing shift so many went through, losing their jobs, losing their homes, or getting caught up in a cash-flow crunch due to the rising cost of credit. This time in history did not benefit the storage business. Many consumers needed storage because of the fallout of the economic mess, but many more stopped using storage because they had to cut back expenses. Consumers were scared. Many did not have the funds to pay for storage. Many current tenants left their spaces because they had to cut back. There was a time when many of the people PhoneSmart sales reps talked to were needing self-storage for a happy reason. They were getting a great new job in a place they always wanted to live. They were building their dream homes. They were renovating their homes. They were helping their kid move into a new home. By the end of 2007, we were talking to very few happy callers. Most were calling because their misfortunes were creating a need for self-storage.

Self-storage benefited from the rise of storage-auction reality television shows. But this publicity did not shine a light on the positive parts of the storage business—only the sad parts.

What kept storage from crashing and what got it back on its feet quickly was a sales culture that drove industry leaders to figure out what the changing consumer needed and wanted and what the changing consumer feared and avoided. Then sales culture practitioners figured out how changes in technology and marketing approaches could help people see real benefit in using storage. New selling and customer service approaches developed quickly. As a result, demand increased and new customers started moving in.

On the one hand, storage saw decreasing occupancy rates and increasing time-on-market rates for their spaces. On the other hand, storage also saw more rental inquiries and a higher conversion rate of inquiries into rentals. It wasn't long before the pace of new rentals overtook the pace of tenants moving out. This adoption of sales culture theory and practice helped self-storage soften its decline and allowed it to quickly bounce back.

Because I led the early adoption of sales culture principles in the storage business, our PhoneSmart unit noticed shifts in customer behavior and demand well before many in the broader economy.

From my narrow viewpoint, I see self-storage as a leading indicator of overall economic conditions in the United States and Canada. My theory held true in this most recent economic crash. In June of 2007, I told the people who ran StorageMart that something was deeply wrong. The 2007 busy season did not happen according to typical patterns from the previous seven seasons. The call waves from incoming phone calls were all wrong. Conversion rates of rental inquiries were down significantly. Consumers were not giving us expected responses to offers, sales talk, and follow ups. We were getting calls from people who were being foreclosed on or evicted. I rang the fire alarm and told everyone in the C suite to move to higher ground and take cover. They double-checked their numbers and indicators and agreed there was an eerie smell in the air. There had been warnings from other sources that the housing market was getting ready to boil over or that the war economy was getting ready to wipe out the civilian economy. The fact that there would be no busy season for storage operators in the summer of 2007 made it clear that the bottom was about to drop. Preparations were made for the scenarios a drop in demand or a crash in the economy might bring.

We redoubled our efforts to figure out how to talk to consumers in their current state of mind. We redoubled marketing efforts. We changed sales processes. We moved ahead of the storm front. We made no secret of what we were doing, so that others in the industry could prepare and adjust. Our actions saved many jobs, preserved an enormous amount of capital, and helped start the economic recovery before many even knew there was an economic meltdown.

The writers of history books twenty-five years from now may also credit self-storage with aiding in the economic recovery in other ways as well. In past economic crashes, people who lost their jobs, homes, or upward mobility often had to abandon everything they owned. There are stories from the Great Depression of entire farms being left behind with all the tools, equipment, and furniture. Photos show furniture strewn along the roads from Oklahoma to California, where so many traveled in an attempt to escape hard times. Songs tell the stories of people who rode the freight rails in search of food or work and who left their homes with nothing but satchels on their backs. The difference between the people in 1932 who stood in bread lines and the people of 2009 who were just scratching by is the ability to put possessions and family heirlooms into a storage unit. A tiny percentage of tenants nowadays have abandoned their units, which made for compelling reality television, but the vast majority of people stored their things for when good times return. Many children born between 1910 and 1935 had nothing to start out with when they left home to become independent adults, just the shoes on their feet, if they were lucky enough to have shoes. How different would things have been if the internally displaced refugees of the Great Depression had been able to leave just a few important things safely in a storage unit while they walked off into the sunset in search of something better?

We all know of a few personal or family stories of the Great Depression. I'll share a few with you in hopes that you remember a few of your own. The stories your kids and grandkids might tell of the economic collapse of 2007–2012 will be very different from these, partly because people were able to preserve their things in a storage unit.

I had a friend as a teenager whose step-grandfather walked to New York City from southern Alabama in the early 1930s to leave the bad times brewing there. Because local authorities along the way harshly treated the people they called vagrants and hobos, and sometimes even lynched the *colored* ones for sport, he walked the rail lines at night and hid during the day, eating scraps and whatever he could beg for or work for when he found a *Negro community* he felt safe in. He arrived in New York with only a blanket and a jackknife, feeling lucky to be alive. He eventually got work delivering coal for a company that serviced apartment buildings in Brooklyn and built a life for himself and his family. I talked to him a few times at family functions, asking him why he had so little on his plate at a family dinner. He remembered the hard times and never wanted to get used to a full belly, so that if hard times came back he wouldn't suffer so much.

I also had a friend from California whose grandparents left west Texas during the Dust Bowl years for the farm fields of California. Everything they had was left behind, abandoned, or bartered away for food along the road. If you've ever seen the classic movie of John Steinbeck's book *The Grapes of Wrath*, you saw their story.

The younger generation whose parents have most recently had their financial stability wiped out, or lost almost everything in the crash, managed to save a lot of furniture, family memories, and items of practical use in a storage unit along one highway or another. It may be that the storage industry will end up taking credit for saving an entire generation's belongings and family traditions.

So if you think you have nothing to learn from the self-storage industry, think again. Perhaps there's a good lesson to learn from the successes self-storage has had in developing a sales culture of its own. Are you with me?

I still haven't told you the first rule of selling. But we are not quite there yet.

Let's concentrate instead on getting a sales culture working in your business. How do you build a sales culture? How do you build any culture? I go to Las Vegas fairly often to trade shows and conferences. Las Vegas is a fascinating place to see because of its powerful gaming culture, at least on the Strip. When you consider the history of Las Vegas, the gaming culture is what created the place and allowed it to diversify into a regional center of commerce, tourism, and development. Once you get off the Strip, you realize that many of the people who live in Las Vegas couldn't care less what happens on the Strip; but everyone in this town lives to some degree or another from the ripples of the gaming culture. So a culture can be very powerful.

How do you create a culture? What makes any kind of culture? If you ever had an interest in anthropology or sociology, then you know that stories, myths, language, rituals, and clothing help create a culture. We have clients in Canada, and a lot of folks think that all you have to do to be a Canadian is just to use a long *o* when you say the word "process" and make the word "about" sound like "a boot." Two simple words, and you are in the Canadian club. (This actually works, by the way.) When we have made *secret shopping* phone calls to Canadian businesses to see how they handle phone calls, we passed for compatriots by talking with a neutral North American accent and adding in the Canadian pronunciation of "process" and "about."

The hip-hop culture, for example, thrives all over the world. You see young people who appear to be into the hip-hop culture, and you think that all you have do to get into the hip-hop culture is just say "yo" and wear baggy, low-riding pants.

Sometimes it can be something very simple that makes someone think you're a member of a culture. I like to wear construction boots and jeans when the weather gets wet and rainy. If it is cold and wet outside, I'll wear my Carhartt jacket and favorite yellow baseball cap, which has a Caterpillar logo on it. I've been taken for a construction worker many times. Now, I suppose I *am* in the construction business from a certain point of view. I construct businesses, sales and marketing processes, and I construct books. But I am not sure I could last a full day on a house framing crew without taking a nap from 2:00 to 4:00 PM.

People are quick to categorize you by the way they see you. You may not like that people don't see you for who you are, but for what they think you are. You may not like to be pigeonholed for the way you might appear or sound. But you can make this work to your benefit. Why do so many professions have a uniform? Because it tells the world clearly who is a firefighter or nurse, so the firefighter or nurse can do their jobs quickly and efficiently.

I did a simple test when I ran a Culligan Bottled Water dealership. I believed that the route drivers were invisible to people and could go where they wanted, when they wanted, without restrictions. One day I went cold-calling for new customers in a business area wearing the water delivery driver's uniform. I wore a striped white and blue shirt and blue shorts. The very next day, I called on the same businesses in a suit and tie. No one recognized me as being the same person. Only a few said that another guy had been through the day before, and no one knew it was me.

I tested my theory further. I walked into a bank, which was not our customer, with a five-gallon bottle on my shoulder and strolled back behind the tellers' counter and back into the break room where I was not supposed to be. No one stopped me. No one asked who I was or where I was going. I had to ask someone in the break room who I should talk to about setting them up with water service before anyone even acknowledged me.

The people in the bank thought I was a member of the service culture and that I was doing something I was supposed to be doing.

I was invisible to them. When I wore the suit and tie, I was identified as a salesman, and the front office people and the receptionists put up a wall of resistance as a result. So we used this set of perceptions to our advantage and dressed all of our salespeople in route driver uniforms. The people we called on in offices and residential neighborhoods did not treat our salespeople with any resistance because the salespeople were seen as members of the service culture. This acceptance, invisibility, and lack of resistance allowed us to build one of the top bottled-water dealerships in the entire Culligan Bottled Water network.

On the other hand, there are definitely times when you want to know who the salesperson is. How do you want your people pigeonholed? Don't you want your customers thinking your people are members of the sales culture? Because don't people love a good sales experience? If you go to a store looking to buy something, doesn't it drive you crazy if the people ignore you, don't help you, and don't help you figure out what to buy? This drives *me* crazy. Let's not do that to our customers. Let's make sure our prospective customers and our current customers see us as members of a sales culture—we are there to help them make their purchases.

What are some of the stories and myths and language we can use to build a sales culture? Let's talk the language of sales. If you talk about suspects and prospects and clients and closing ratios and things of that nature, your staff starts thinking like salespeople. If you start talking like salespeople, you start thinking like salespeople.

Perhaps these concepts are foreign to you, so I'll run through a few phrases.

A *suspect* is someone you hope might, maybe, could, or should do business with you. In many businesses, you actually don't talk to suspects unless you knock on doors in the neighborhood.

The people who call you on the phone and the people who walk into your place are *prospects* because they've identified that they either have a need or think a need is coming up. Prospects express a need or desire for what you have to offer.

Closing ratios or *conversion ratios* tell you how many prospects it takes you to get a customer. These ratios can change dramatically based on where your prospects come from. In self-storage you typically get prospects from people who see your location from traveling by it, Internet users who see your website, mobile phone users using review or map apps, referrals from current customers, repeat customers, mailers, fliers, and other marketing efforts. Your business has its own sources of prospects. You should know all of these sources and their closing ratios, so you can better manage your efforts and better judge when you are doing something right or when you are missing the mark. The advancement of analytic and business intelligence software has made it virtually impossible to not know where your customers come from, how they find you, and how they convert.

Learn the vocabulary of selling and then talk about the process of selling. Talk about *qualifying questions* such as, "Do you know how soon you're going to need a (fill in the blank with something you sell)?" "Do you have an idea of what size you need, or can I help you figure that?" "Do you know where we're located, and is that a good location for you?" "Would you like a table, or would you prefer a seat at the bar?" Design and frame your qualifiers intentionally.

Are you familiar with *closing questions*? If you use the term in your business, do you actually ask closing questions to your prospects? "When would you like to move in?" "Is Saturday a good time for you to come in or is Sunday better?" "Would you like the breakfast menu or are you having lunch?" If your people understand what closing questions are, they'll use them, and your culture will develop.

I have heard some people call a closing question "the ask." This is not a bad concept. When you get to the right point in your conversation with your prospect, and you have asked good qualifying questions, it is time for the ask. You ask the person to make the purchase.

I have heard others say that using the term "close" sounds crude and adversarial, as if your prospect might get hurt when you *close* them. This is not a bad point either. Maybe you are really asking people to *open* an account with you or to *open* a business relationship with you. I like this way of thinking. It shines a positive light on the way in which you ask someone to be your customer.

Other selling organizations say that you should never *ask* for a sale, you should always *assume* a sale. There is a big difference between a car salesman saying, "Can I write up the red Mustang for you?" and "Let's get the red Mustang written up for you so you can take it home tonight."

Do you see what is happening here? By talking about sales issues in the language of selling, we are participating in the culture of sales. Help your people be in the culture of sales by talking about selling.

Talk about some of the cost issues. A sales culture knows what it takes to make money. What does it actually cost you to get a new business inquiry? Do you know what a telephone call costs your business? Have you done the math? You would be shocked to see how much it costs to actually make the phone ring. Now take that one step further and figure out what each telephone inquiry costs you. Use your marketing and advertising budget to figure out how many actual phone call inquiries you generate. Take another step to figure out where these telephone inquiries come from. People are getting your phone number from many different sources. If you knew all those sources and the power of each of them, it would shake you up! Despite the cost and importance of telephone inquiries, many businesses get very few new business inquiries. Do they count in your business? Don't they make each phone call, each walk-in customer, or each email even that much more important?

What is happening with your online visitors? Your analytics packages should be able to tell you all about who they are, what they do on your site, and how they either become customers or abandon you.

What does it actually cost you for an acquisition? Can you segment out each of your sources and get a close estimate on what each class of customers costs? You may find some of your most expensive types of customers to acquire are your shortest-lived customers. Maybe they are your longest clients? How can you drive that cost lower? How do you find more of the customers that are less expensive? How can you capture some of the opportunities that you're not catching? Talking about the costs associated with opening new accounts makes your staff think like salespeople.

One of the sales topics I like to talk about is the idea of *concerns and assurances*. Are you familiar with the terms "objections" and "rebuttals"? These are ways of talking about the reasons people do not buy and the things we can do or say to overcome a reason for not buying. Do you like the terms *objection* and *rebuttal*? They sound like something that happens in a courtroom during a dispute over facts. It sounds rude to give a rebuttal to your prospect. It sounds adversarial. You often have to fight to win a customer, but I don't think you should be fighting with the potential customer. Making a decision to buy is not an act of submission to the salesperson. Our prospects don't come in and say, "I object to what you are offering me. I will not submit!" What they do is say to themselves, "I'm not sure about this. I'm not sure about that. I'm not sure about something else." They have concerns about making a good decision.

So if your salespeople are great at assuring your potential clients that they are making a good choice when they do business with you, then you've made the sale, and you've made great strides in creating your sales culture.

Your sales culture succeeds when its main focus is helping people realize that it is comfortable to decide to buy from you.

I'll give you a million-dollar tip. There's a wonderful method of assuring customers that your offering is a good choice. It is called the "feel-felt-found." And you're all using this method now to a certain extent whether or not you know it. There are other ancient and reliable sales methods you are using in your business that already have names and have been handed down from one generation of salespeople to the next, just like the stories and traditions of other cultures. Only you may not know their names or how to use them correctly. I am here to help you get in touch with the roots of the culture of selling. I'll help you by telling you about feel-felt-found.

Feel-felt-found goes like this: "I understand how you feel about spending that much money on our ergonomic yoga chair. Some of our other customers felt that way, too, before they moved their new chairs into their offices. What they found after using our chair was they were so much more energetic at the end of the day, and their back and hip pains were significantly reduced. They now feel this was the best money they ever spent. That's why a large portion of our business comes from referrals. Did you want your chair in leather or vinyl?"

That's how the feel-felt-found works, and it works with every concern that people have when they talk to you. "I understand how you feel about the price of our flooring. Some of our customers felt like it was a lot of money, too, before ordering our flooring, but what they found was that with the ease of care and natural beauty our flooring offers, they were very, very happy. So I can assure you you're going to be very happy with the installation. Would you like us to deliver today, or would tomorrow be better for you?" It's a powerful technique. You can customize it to your own way of speaking, and you can use it all day long and never get tired of it.

Do not look at the things preventing a prospect from saying, "Sure, I'll buy from you now" as objections. They are only concerns. Treat them as concerns.

Another sales issue that is important to talk about is the concept and the practice of follow-up. We'd like to think that prospects make up their mind quickly and decide to buy within a few days of deciding they might need something from us. The fact is that there are many different time frames for different classes of prospects. You can sell to perhaps 30 percent of the people you talk to today in the future, even when they cannot make a decision today. Even if you did everything in your power to help them decide today, they can't all decide today. That said, you need to make sure you aren't letting your competitors sell to lots of your prospects because you are letting those prospects get away from you. Do you think you are doing follow-up very well? Come up with an ideal follow-up system to make sure that everyone you talk to either purchases from you now or purchases from you later—your prospects may not be shoppers, but they are often buyers. They don't stop at your place of business because they think the flowerbed out in front is pretty. They stop because they have a need or their spouses told them they're going to have a need. People may browse the Internet to research your business or the types of services and products you offer. But they do not call you on the phone or stop by your location to kill time. They are buyers. So they're either going to buy from you, or you are going to let them buy from someone else, or perhaps their situation is going to change, and they're not going to buy from anyone. So get a follow-up system in place. It is what a sales culture would do.

What are some of the goals and targets you need to promote with your staff? Some of them are fairly obvious such as production goals.

But does your staff know you're looking at a variety of metrics that drive revenue? Do they know the difference between them and how they influence your business? What about revenue goals? Does your staff understand that when it's time for price increases, it is okay to lose a few customers? You have work to build your sales culture, so they understand the goals and targets you're shooting at.

Do you have functional systems for cross-selling, up-selling, and reselling? Does anyone even talk about these topics at your workplace? Many times when I am traveling, I will have a coffee and a muffin for a quick breakfast. I love watching the pros at the well-established coffee shops move people through the line. They're fantastic. They move you through that line fast. That part is wonderful. But what they don't do is up-sell. When they ask you, "Yes, can I help you? What would you like?" and you say, "I'd like a coffee and a muffin," they don't often say, "Would you like a Danish too?" or "Would you like a second muffin to take with you for later?" If they did ask, and if every third person took them up on the offer of the Danish or second muffin, they could be looking at a 15 to 20 percent boost in revenue.

But they've got the system of moving people through the shop quickly down pat. So is that what you have at your company? Do you have a great way to move people in quickly and efficiently but forget to sell your full range of products?

What are some of your revenue targets, and do your people know what your revenue targets are? Get them on the team. I assure you, the entire offensive line of a football team knows what they have to do during a game: They have to give the quarterback enough time to get his aim right. They have to block right on some plays, block left on others, and let the defensive players through the line on yet other plays. They know their roles in every play in the book. Does your staff even know there is a playbook for your business? How can you build stories and myths about the great plays that have been made by your people, if they don't even know there is a playbook?

Let's talk about some of the myths and stories that build a culture. Do you know any kids who have seen many of the Disney movies? These movies help lay the foundation of popular American culture. A kid who hasn't seen *High School Musical, Cinderella,* or

Finding Nemo or at least *The Lion King* is not in our culture. He or she might as well live on the moon!

If Disney tells the stories that help build our pop culture, what kind of myths, rules, and stories help build a sales culture? Let's think about that for a minute. One of the rules I love is called the "rule of thirds." There's actually a rule of thirds for many different kinds of situations because it is easy to remember three things, and it is easy to draw a triangle. Here's how our rule of thirds goes: one group of people is going to buy from you anyway, no matter what, as long as you don't say something stupid or chase them off, because they've already decided they like your business. In the storage business, these people know someone who's rented there. Maybe they drive by it every day and think it looks good. Whatever the reason is, they've already decided they're going to rent from that location, and when they come in to see the place or call on the phone, what they're really trying to find out is if they *shouldn't* rent from that location. In their minds, they are asking themselves if their inclination to rent there is wrong. So when you get someone in this easy third, your job is to not drive them off and to just let them buy.

You have another group of people who aren't going to buy from you anyway no matter what you do because their situation is going to change. If it was a storage prospect, perhaps the house doesn't sell, the divorce doesn't happen, and they reconcile. The situation changes. Their uncle Fred says, "Don't pay for storage. I've got a barn you can use for free." Something will happen to those people; you'll lose them without any wrongdoing of your own. Your job with those people is to give them as good an experience as you can so when it is time for them to actually need what you offer, they'll think of you and contact you first.

But then there is the third group of people that could go either way. They're not quite sure what they're doing. They're not quite sure they're going to buy. They're not quite sure they're going to spend the money. They're not quite sure they like your place. They're not quite sure they can afford your place. The people that can go either way are those who help you make money. They make your money because they represent the *upside* in your promotional spending.

Anyone who is halfway friendly can sell to that easy third, but only people with sales skills and persistence and people who see themselves in a sales culture can work with the third that can go either way. If you can convert a nice share of that either-way third, those dollars go right to your bottom line. The people you might not have sold to before you adopted a sales culture are those who represent your increase in revenue. So keep the rule of thirds in mind when you're talking to prospects. Is this person in the easy third? If so, just let this person buy from you. Is this person in the impossible third? I'll give you an example of an impossible third.

We received a certain phone call at our PhoneSmart call center. One of our supervisors, Dana, was catching calls for our many self-storage clients. She asked the caller, "How soon are you going to need a storage unit?" and he said, "I'm retiring in four years. I won't need it until then, but I'm just curious what one costs." So there's a prepared man! He's certainly in the impossible third because no matter how great you are at sales and service, he is not going to retire this week just to start renting his storage unit from you.

You then talk to all of the other people who say, "I still have to shop around," "That's maybe a little more than I'm looking to spend," "I'm not sure if I'm ready to do anything yet," "I've got to check with my boss," and "I've got to check with my spouse." When you can sell to a large portion of these people, that's when you make your money.

Here is another rule of selling I like. It's called the "chuckle rule," and it goes like this: for every chuckle you share with a prospect, the odds of you doing business together doubles. It's an exponential formula. If you get one chuckle, your odds are twice as good. If you get two chuckles, the odds are four times as good. Now there's a point of diminishing returns in there somewhere around the third to fifth chuckle where the people are laughing so hard, they leave your store, or they have had enough and would like to get down to business. But keep the chuckle rule in mind. It's an important rule because that moment of laughter gives you great rapport with people. Having that rapport allows you to talk openly and honestly with them. It means they are likely to follow your recommendations. It means you can be assertive in dealing with them.

I spoke to one of our self-storage clients recently who told me about how the chuckle rule helped him make a rental. Someone walked into the store, and they shared a few laughs. The potential customer told our client he was not ready to rent anything yet and started to walk out the door. Our client, the store manager, said, "Oh, come on now, you know you're going to need it Saturday. Isn't the best thing to just get it today and start getting organized before Saturday?" and the guy turned around and said, "Yeah, you're probably right. Okay." Not the most sophisticated close in the world, but it worked because he shared a few chuckles and established a rapport. He didn't have to be particularly smooth when he tried one more time to get the rental. He just had to try. The chuckle rule is a powerful technique.

I haven't told you the first rule of selling yet, but I am getting close. Let's talk more about sales stories.

Stories are a great way to foster a culture. There are some great stories that can help your staff relate to selling. Did you ever go ice fishing? Did you ever live up north where you *can* go ice fishing? I lived in Wisconsin as a kid, and not only did we ice fish, but it was lots of fun to drive our cars around on the lakes. If you are not accustomed to the ice culture, you might say, "What, are you guys nuts?" and I'd say, "Well, yes, but the ice was thick!" There are, of course, stories about people who went out on the ice a day too early or a day too late in the season. More than a few cars and snowmobiles are at the bottom of Wisconsin lakes.

Greg Tyler, a storyteller from Columbia, Missouri, has many wonderful stories to share, such as this one, which is part of the oral tradition of the sales culture. If you like this one, please pass it on to your staff.

If you know a bit about ice fishing, you know it is its own culture, and you can buy as much gear for ice fishing as you can for anything else. There was this one guy who bought all of the gear. He had the fancy icehouse that he could pull out on a trailer with his TV and DVD player in there, with a heater and satellite connection. He had his automatic fish finder, his power auger to get through the ice, and the most expensive ice-fishing pole. He sat there one day in his cozy hut, watching TV with his hook down in the water. Nothing happened. Not a single nibble. He looked out the double-paned-insulated glass of his fishing hut and saw a little kid walk up to a spot in the ice not too far away, with a bucket in his hand and a hatchet. The kid turned the bucket upside down, sat down on the bucket, took the hatchet and chopped a little hole in the ice, and threw a string with a hook down in there. The guy in the fancy ice hut watched for a little while because he thought it was pretty funny. He started ice fishing the same way when he was a kid. He laughed, thinking of how frustrated the kid would be sitting out in the freezing cold on his bucket all day trying to catch one fish. Our friend in the fancy icehouse was eager to start piling up all the fish his expensive gear would help him catch and was about to go back to his ice hole, when the kid pulled a fish out, and the guy chuckled. He thought, *Isn't that cute? Beginner's luck*. The guy then noticed he felt annoyed because he had already been out there for a while, and he had nothing to show for it.

He sat back down at his ice hole and flipped to the golf channel on his satellite TV. Just then, out of the corner of his eye, he saw the kid pull another fish out of the lake. And then another one. Now the guy was starting to get more than annoyed because his $6,000 fish finder wasn't helping him. So he got out of his 72-degree icehouse, walked over to the kid, and said, "Hey, kid, what's your secret?" and the kid said, "Mum ah mum mum." The guy had no idea what he said and thought to himself, *Oh, great! The kid is special ed too!* He turned around to go back to his icehouse, threw his hook in again, and nothing happening. Not a nibble. He sat there for a few minutes, which seemed like an hour. He looked out the window again; the kid had three more fish up on the ice. Now the guy was mad. He walked over to the kid and said, "Kid, I've got to know your secret." The kid said, "MUM AH MUM MUM," and the guy said, "Look, kid, I can't understand your gibberish. You've got to tell me, what's your secret?" So the kid held up his hand to his mouth, spat some worms out into his hand, and said quite matter of factly, "Keep your bait warm!"

You can imagine that our friend with all the fancy gear stood humbled for at least a moment or two.

What do you do to keep the bait warm in your business? Do you have a warm, friendly smile when people come in? Are you sure to make an extra walk around your property to see that there's no litter floating around your place? Are you constantly checking your website to make sure your user experience is top-notch? Are you keeping your bait warm, or are you relying on your gadgets and expensive advertising and concessions to bring you business?

Here's another good story about selling. Have you ever worked in retail? I worked in a toy store during the Christmas holidays one year while I was in high school, so I can relate to some of the challenges of helping retail customers.

There was this young guy right out of high school who went to work for a fantastic department store—not your normal department store; it was like Penney's and Dillard's and Cabela's and Walmart and an auto mall all wrapped into one. Everything you could possibly imagine was there. The owner took an interest in all of the new people and came down from the office to introduce himself to the kid. He said, "I hope you have a good first day" and went back up to the office. At the end of the day, the owner went downstairs to see how the kid had done. He said, "Well, kid, how did you do today? How many customers did you help?" And the kid said, "I . . . I helped one customer today." The owner starts getting red in the face, "You were here all day, and you helped *one* customer? What did you sell him?" "I sold him a fishing hook." (I like fishing stories!)

So the owner said, "You sold him a fishing hook?" and the kid said, "Yes, and then after that we found out he didn't have a rod and reel, so we went over and picked him out the latest new reel with the luxury rod and got him a whole big tackle box full of all of the stuff he'd need." And the owner went, "Okay, that's good. Is that all you sold him?" and the kid said, "No, no. We found out he didn't have any outdoor clothes, so we went over to the outdoor clothes department and got him waders and a big coat and some camo gear while we were at it and some new boots. He looked real sharp. And then we found out he didn't have a fishing boat, so we went over to the boat department and picked him out a beautiful boat that was going to be just right for what he wanted to do. But he didn't have a trailer, so we had to add a trailer to that. And then we found out that he drove over here this morning in his little Volkswagen Jetta and couldn't haul anything with it. So we went over to the truck department and got him a new GMC 3500 dual-wheel on-demand four-wheel-drive super-torque, and he drove off."

By this time the owner's jaw was to the ground. He said, "This is incredible! You sold all of this to a guy who came in looking for a fishing hook?" And the kid said, "Well, actually, I was working in the pharmacy early this morning, and he came in looking for aspirin, and I happened to say to him, "It would be a nice weekend to go fishing, don't you think?"

If this isn't a good example of suggestive selling, I don't know what is.

How many times do you have people come in to your business, call you on the phone, or email you just to ignore them? Or how many times do people come in to buy from you, and you forget that they're going to need other things to make that purchase a happy one? You forget about people from time to time; you get busy and forget to take an extra second with a customer. Does your website let someone buy one item without showing them other items that will match? How many times have you talked to someone on the phone and given her your store hours and then realized that you've hung up without asking if she needed to buy something? Don't let it happen again. You are giving away money every time you do that.

Share these stories with your people, all of which will help them get into the mindset of being in selling mode and being *on* with their sales techniques. This allows you, then, to track things such as personal bests. Do you even have legends in your company about the day that someone sold ten units to the same customer, or when so-and-so reserved twenty-seven units in a day? There are fantastic feats of selling that happen in your company. Find them! Celebrate them! Have some fun with them! Some of them are admirable, and they're just fun to think about.

Look for those wonderful feats of salesmanship. There have been people who came in to your office and were mad at you about an issue, and you ended up selling them something anyway. There have been people who went to buy from your competitor after talking to you and then showed up the next day at your place wanting to buy from you instead. Stories like this are wonderful stories to tell.

Cultures also have rules. There are rules in selling. Some are unwritten, and some may already be up on the wall in your office. What kind of written and unwritten rules do you have in your sales culture?

One rule might be to get up from the desk and come around the counter to greet people when they come in to your store. One rule might be if you have two people at the counter you're dealing with and the phone rings, you let it ring instead of trying to talk on the phone and in person at the same time.

Another great rule, perhaps the oldest rule of selling, is "Close early and often." If someone calls you up and asks, "Do you have any X available?" do you say, "Sure! How soon would you like it?" If you do close early and often, I salute you! If the first words out of your mouth are a closing question, you are fantastic.

How do you establish selling rules in your culture? Do you write them down? Do you practice them? Do you drill them?

A sales culture also deliberately uses customer incentives, promotions, and giveaways. It's not a bad idea to always give something away to bring in business. It doesn't have to be of great value. It doesn't have to cost you much, but it does bring goodwill if you give away something every now and then. Look at how a free toy built a burger chain.

A sales culture also finds a way to make its location a destination for its customers. What do you have that makes people stop in? I know a storage operator who always has fresh cookies out on the counter. He has people he hasn't rented to in years stop by to get cookies when they're running around town. His customers stop in the office just to have a snack. Whatever it takes for you to make your store a destination for people will help you build your business. You don't have to go to the lengths Disney has gone to become a destination, but you do need to find what is appropriate for your business.

When Krispy Kreme powers up the hot light, people swarm from miles around to get their hot donuts. Krispy Kreme has become a destination that calls in people by switching on a light. What are you doing?

You don't need a roller coaster or a marching band, but you need something fun that people appreciate.

Another way to establish and develop your sales culture is to follow your scripting. A lot of people don't like scripts. That is because a lot of people do not develop good scripts or use them correctly. Let me suggest how to use scripting properly.

Scripting should never be paragraphs; scripting should be phrases or easily digestible sentences. Salespeople have to be able to express the gist of your scripting in their own words. If you have your people memorize some fantastic phrases for qualifying questions and closing questions and let them fill in all of the rest with their normal conversation, it will turn out as friendly, concerned conversation. If you want your people to do word-for-word scripting in sentences and paragraphs, they won't be able to do it. They'll trip over it. They'll sound canned. They'll sound uncomfortable, and they'll chase your prospects away. Instead, master phrases. Master certain questions, and let that be your scripting.

When developing your script, concentrate on hitting specific points, crossing certain thresholds, and asking for the business. This can be done many different ways. When done so it sounds conversational, you will make a lot more sales and create a lot more referrals.

Another great rule of selling is to stay away from the word "if." Say "when" instead. Don't tell your prospect, "If you rent from us, you'll find that it's a great experience." Instead, say, "When you're one of our tenants, you'll like staying here because—" Do the assumptive selling.

We'll deal more with how to assume the sale later. If you can do it well in your organization, you will find your sales culture will thrive.

Learning to close a sale is also key to building your sales culture. Use your alternate-choice close. Are you familiar with the alternate-choice close as a standard selling technique? You actually use it all of the time or have had it used on you. You walk into a store to look for an item, and the sales clerk asks, "Did you want that in red or green?" You hear it all of the time. You go to the restaurant, "Smoking or nonsmoking?" Your kids want to go to the movies, and they say, "Hey, Dad, let's go to the movies. They've got a show at seven and one at nine. Which one do you want to go to?" It's powerful stuff. Teach it to your people and learn it and use it all of the time. Your business probably has many excellent alternative choices built into it. Find them and use them.

Seek out good examples of sales cultures and talk about them with your staff. Photo studios are a good example of a great sales culture. When was the last time you took your family to a photo studio for family pictures? How many times have you walked in there thinking, *Mmm, I'll probably spend X dollars on a package,* and how many times have you actually have walked out of there spending what you intended to spend? It's always two or three times more, isn't it? Always. And aren't you happy you did it? Were you mad? If you were mad, it lasted until Grandma saw the pictures and went "Ohhhh!" How do the photographers do it? With assumptive selling. You show up, and they know you're not there to look at a picture and go home; you're there to buy pictures. So everything they do is assumptive selling.

And they're masters of the alternate-choice close. They take several different poses, then they show you the pictures and say, "Of Pose A, which is your favorite picture of Pose A? Is it this picture or that picture?" You pick one, and they put it to the side. "Let's look at Pose B; which one do you like best there, number one, two, or three?" You go, "Well, I don't like number three." "Okay, let's forget three. How about number one or two? Number two looks good, doesn't it?" "Yes, it does." "Okay, great!" Now you've got another one. And they go through every pose until they've alternate-choice closed you into a seven-page package. You can't say no. Are you going to say, "No, I don't want gorgeous pictures of my lovely children!" You can't say it... well, some people could, but it's very hard to. Especially when they're sitting right next to you and listening to you. The people in the photo studio business are masters of a sales culture.

And then they've got seventeen different payment options. So if you try to get out of one by saying, "Well, you know, I don't have that much with me—" they'll say, "Oh, well, no problem!" because you can do this option, this option, or the other option. They're masters of it.

Look at other businesses you deal with that are masters of the sales culture, and then think about how well you master it in your company. Are you really mastering it, or are you just skating? Take a look and see what you think.

As you develop your culture, you will have challenges to face. How do you find people to participate in your culture? I mentioned the hip-hop culture. You can't join the hip-hop culture unless you like a booming baseline. First prerequisite: If you don't like your head vibrating from the bass line, you can't join the hip-hop culture. Every culture has prerequisites.

So let's talk about sales culture. How do you find filtering systems to filter out the people who don't belong? Perhaps you have tried to train someone who wasn't really interested in being in a sales culture and had a bad experience. It is probably because you did not establish the prerequisites and hire accordingly.

Let's look for qualifying hoops. How do you find the people you hire? If you're using advertisements, how do you *word* those advertisements? What do you call your position? Is your position a salesperson? Is your position a store manager? Whatever you call it now, I urge you to call it something different in your next advertising campaign, call it something different in the next one, and keep playing with wording and find out what sort of people are attracted by what sort of ad you run for the position. It's interesting to find out what happens. We do this when we hire at PhoneSmart. Sometimes we call the PhoneSmart rep's job a "call center position." Sometimes we call it "inbound sales." Sometimes we call it "marketing." We try so many different things just to see what people are attracted to. It's fascinating to see the results.

You should also do voice screening for prospective employees. Do you hate to hire people because you have to talk to seventy-five people to get two that you want to interview? It's frustrating, isn't it? So what's the one way that people judge your staff? Let's say they're calling on the phone; how much time do you think your staff has to make a great impression on the caller? Five seconds? Ten seconds? So why not set up a voice-mail message, so your new prospective hires call in on the voice message. Your greeting will invite them to talk to you for a minute and tell you something about themselves. You give them twenty seconds; if they have a smile in their voice and you enjoy how they sound, call them up and do a telephone interview. If not, delete the message and move on to the next one. It's coldhearted, but your customers don't give your people more than five or ten seconds to impress them. So use that as a yardstick.

Certainly look for the red flags and the green flags. What are those? They can be all kinds of different things. Some people certainly don't like hiring people who've had lots of jobs, but I caution you to not automatically eliminate someone because of that. Sometimes what you see is a progression in responsibility or a person who has a goal to be at a certain level and keeps having to move through organizations to get to that level. So just because they've had a lot of jobs doesn't mean they go to work the first week and then oversleep every day and get fired. That's not what it always means. You have to look deeper into that subject.

Look at your prospective employee's online profile. You may find very little online about someone, or you may find out more than you'd care to know. You need to know who you are bringing to your team.

Green flags should come up when people are fun to talk to, when people have engaging smiles, and when people are enjoyable to visit with. A green flag should come up if a potential hire is a good storyteller or asks you pertinent questions about the position. It is tempting to hire people you think you could be friends with, though I caution you not to hire your friends or people who look like potential friends because that can be complicated. You *should* hire people you enjoy talking to because your customers will enjoy talking to them too. Hire people who make a great first impression on you because they will make a good impression on customers. Hire people your customers could make friends with.

You should *secret shop* your potential recruits. There are easy ways you can do this. If you're looking at a résumé, and you see where the person is working, especially if it's a retail shop, go down there to buy something to see how you're treated. It will tell you tons. Call her on the phone. Ask questions about whatever her business is. It may seem a little secret agent-ish, but it's going to save you a lot of time and trouble. You need to know what sort of a company culture your new hire currently lives in. You need to know if your new hire acts like the right person for your budding sales culture. Having the right person working in your company will make a huge difference to you. It's just a matter of finding those people.

What does work history tell you? I'm not a huge fan of résumés. I have to apologize to the educational system and people who create résumés. Education and work history can be interesting or can give a certain background, but the quality of the individual is what means the most. That does not show up on paper. Résumés are interesting;

they're a way to spark conversation, but they don't necessarily tell you what that person is capable of, what they can do in a pinch, or if they can think on their feet. You've got to find that out in different ways. Test for these abilities.

I like to boil this whole process for bringing people into your sales culture down to two acid tests you have to pass on a day-to-day basis when selling. These two tests tell you how a person's natural disposition will direct them to look for a sale every time they talk to someone, and if they ask for the sale every time. When it's busy, and they are tired and the company is short-staffed, how does the person in question handle basic selling attitude? There are two killer phrases you can use when secret shopping a potential employee or when evaluating current employees: "How late are you open today?" and "That's more than I am looking to spend."

If someone calls your business and asks, "How late are you open today?" how will your people respond? If your response to that is not something like, "What time did you want to come in? We have some great offers today," you're sunk. If your response is, "Oh, we're open until six," and you hang up, you will fail in your efforts to build a sales culture. Ask for the sale every time. The response to this phrase tells you if the person in question is always in selling mode. When real people call your business and ask this question, they want to know that you want to sell them something.

The next killer phrase is, "That's a little more than I'm looking to spend." The whole issue of price is like a poker game. When people tell you, "Oh, that's a little more than I'm looking to spend," they're looking to see if they can negotiate pricing with you. They're looking to see if you have confidence in your pricing. Because if you don't have confidence in your pricing, they will think you're charging too much and ripping them off. When someone says, "Oh, that's a little more than I'm looking to spend," if you say, "Oh," and have no way to justify the price, you're sunk! How your people answer the price concern also determines whether you sell to enough people in the could-go-either-way category. If a potential recruit has no good response to this killer phrase, you have work to do to get that person's head into the selling game. If you are unsure of how to handle the price discussion, keep on reading.

If the people you hire are able to deal with these killer phrases on a busy day when they're tired, and you are short-staffed, you've got the right people.

We can use PhoneSmart as a case study. We use a voice-mail message for prospective hires with great success. When someone calls in off of a help-wanted promotion, they hear a greeting that tells a lot about what we do, a lot about what we're looking for, and it invites callers to tell us about themselves. When listening to the callers on the employment hotline, we usually give them about twenty or thirty seconds. If you can hear them smiling, if they're having fun with it—because a lot of times, it's embarrassing for them—then we keep listening. They don't realize that when they call you, they're doing an audio audition until they get the message. So you get to hear real stuff. It will catch some people off-guard, and you can hear how good they are at recovery. Since they are often not prepared for what to say, you get natural responses that tell you about this person's natural tendencies. If we like what we hear, we save the message and call those we like back to set up a telephone interview.

It is interesting that sometimes when you call people back who sounded great on the message, they answer the phone at their houses by saying, "What?" We are quick to say, "Oops! Sorry!" and get off the phone. When you call the people back, you catch them being themselves and can hear whether they have good speaking skills, if they can think on their feet, and if they can improvise. Those are all fantastic talents to have in a new staff person.

We eliminate many people during a telephone interview. Our core selling and customer service work are done by phone. If someone isn't a great phone talker, we cannot have them on the team.

It is also important to hire people who have the natural tendency to be patient and friendly because when it's slow at your office, anybody could handle the customers. No problem. But when it gets busy, can your staff maintain its composure and act in a friendly and professional manner with everyone? We experience slow and busy times in our business. We see this in our call volume reports. It is probably not peculiar to any industry. Our experience is that no one in the whole hemisphere seems to want to rent a storage unit for any give hour on any given day, and then everybody and their brother wants one at the same time. You may get peaks and valleys like that in your business too. You'll sit there with your chin in your hand for a while, like the Maytag man, and then all of a sudden you've got five people at the counter, and the phone won't stop ringing. So how do you test to see if prospective hires can stay friendly and patient in a pinch like this?

One of the tests we've come up with for composure and patience is "The Break Room Test." When someone comes in for a live interview, we sit that person in the break room for a few minutes. We say, "I'm sorry, the person who's interviewing you is running a little bit late. She'll be right there," and then we'll leave the person in there for five or ten minutes. One of the staff will walk through and in passing say, "Hello," to see if that person's natural response is to say hello back in a friendly way. If the potential hire doesn't respond in a friendly way, that's a short interview. If the person in the break room starts getting impatient and annoyed, that's a short interview. We may leave the person sitting there even longer to make sure. Another staff person may come in and apologize for an additional delay while we see what happens next. We leave reading materials about our company and industry in the break room. If the person being tested leafs through the material, then we feel good about their curiosity and ability to use downtime to learn something they might need. Oftentimes, employees are taking their breaks while a potential hire is sitting in there with them. It is also interesting to see how a potential hire reacts to that. Sometimes the new person will strike up a conversation with someone. Sometimes a new hire becomes uncomfortable. I can't tell you how many times we've saved ourselves from a bad hire by doing this. We regularly have people who sound great on the phone and talk a good game in the telephone interview fail the break room test. You might agree that a lot of people interview very well, and then after you've had them on staff for a couple of weeks, you think they've become a different person or sometimes even their evil twin is working for you. The break room test is a way you can find people who are patient and friendly.

Another interesting and important result of hiring in this manner is a diverse and varied workforce. Our people work on the phone, so their physical appearance or adherence to a particular lifestyle or fashion sense has nothing to do with how customers perceive them. Since we only care how well people sound on the phone, how well-suited they are to live in a sales culture, and how well they get along with people, our employee demographics are broad and varied. Your customer base or selling environment may require a physical appearance standard or a uniform. For instance, you may not be able to hire people with face tattoos or nose piercings. None of that sort of thing matters in the least to us. This gives us a huge edge in hiring talented salespeople. You might also consider what does not matter in the least to your hiring requirements and use that to your advantage when recruiting.

Put yourself in your candidate's position. Job interviews stink! They're terrible to go to because you never know what the people doing the hiring are looking for. You are worried if they like you or don't like you. It is awkward to be looked at with judging eyes. Who really wants a job anyway? Work is overrated as it is. It's a pressurized situation in which you can see whether people can maintain their nerve and composure under duress.

In the positions you fill and the positions we fill, people have to use computers, phones, and software. So we run potential hires through a little test to make sure they can talk, type, and read at the same time. You might think that everyone can do basic keyboarding, manage basic software, and use a piece of telephone equipment, but not everyone can do all three at the same time. You need to know that you have people who can run your management software and fix the glitches. You have some things you need to test for too. Develop a test that will tell you if the person can learn what needs to be done.

Of course, you have to test for selling skills. Hopefully you have recognized some good selling and questioning skills in the phone interview, but you need to know the prospective hire can sell your products and services. The oldest, silliest, but still effective way of testing someone's selling skills is to grab the thing nearest to you and ask the person you are interviewing to sell it to you. "Okay, why don't you just sell me this box of Tic Tacs?" Or "How would you sell me this pen?" You put people in a terribly uncomfortable spot, and you'll see how they sell under pressure. What you'll find is there are a lot of people who have great natural selling skills, and they'll ask questions to determine how best to approach you. When they do that, you have somebody you can work with. And then there are people who have backward selling skills who think that what they have to do to sell something to you is to hit you over the head with whatever they are selling. "These are great Tic Tacs. You need them. You should buy them." That's probably not the approach you want. This hit 'em over the head style shows initiative and energy but not skill. Can you teach a skill to someone whose natural tendency is to fall back to the pushy technique? Perhaps you can. Perhaps you cannot. You need to think about what hoops your potential hires need to jump through before you are comfortable letting them be responsible for your multimillion-dollar assets and revenue goals.

And seeing *is* believing. I recommend if you're not doing it now, to hire people on a probationary period. Use them on a temporary project. Hire them on a test basis. See what happens. Give them a chance to get a feel for your organization because being a salesperson in your business is not for everyone. Most positions involve wearing a lot of hats and mastering many different tasks. Just because someone's good at one or two things doesn't mean they're good at enough of them that you want to keep them on staff. So set a temporary assignment with them or start them part-time.

If you can't hire for a short project or part-time, then you are going to have to get very good with your selection process to make sure your stick-rate of new people is good. You're going to have to get good at training new people to make sure the well-qualified people you hire become successful. Set daily goals or milestones for your trainees, so they and you know if someone had a good day and can move on to the next step.

Give them increasing responsibility as they pass the day-to-day tests. Bring them on slowly because, no matter what your new position is, it's overwhelming in the beginning. Usually at the end of the first week, the people are in a fog, and you need to give them a day or two to settle down from that. Starting slowly also allows you to avoid committing to something that you're going to need to wiggle out of later. It is better to have a set probationary period, so if the hire does not work out, you have a graceful exit. You can simply choose not to keep them on, or you can decline to make a permanent offer.

If you still like the hire after the probationary period, it's much better to say, "Do you know what? I'm happy I hired you. This is working great. Are you happy here too?" Then they can say, "Yes, I like it." You don't want to be put in the position where you hire someone off the bat on a permanent basis and then find out in thirty days you shouldn't have hired this person. Then you have to fire them. That's not fun.

Pay attention to where you're going to take the people you hire because the sky is the limit. Some people have a lot more potential in them than you see in the first couple weeks. Be prepared to develop that potential. Give new hires tasks that will interest them. Let them develop themselves. That's how great salespeople become great salespeople. They are given the latitude to develop. So if you see someone has that potential, let that person develop. Later on you can let them train the next level of new people. At the same time, do not punish people who do not want to move up. For many of your people, the job you hired them to do works perfectly for what they need. They do not need nor do they want more. Help them to get the most and make the most of that position.

But be cautious about how you judge your new hires. Until you get to know them, you may make assumptions about them that make it hard for them to succeed. In the end it is easier and more effective to take into account your employees' individuality than it is to make everyone adhere to one set of guidelines. I'll give you a good example. We almost fired a fantastic rep of ours, and here's what happened. She did all of the initial testing great. She did well in the initial training program. She was a college student, and we had her work in the evenings. Unfortunately, after a month or so on the regular schedule, her numbers just weren't that good. We couldn't figure it out because she knew what to do, she had the personality, but we were thinking maybe we made a hiring mistake. Sometimes with college students, work is their fifth or sixth priority in life, and that is not always acceptable to you as the employer. You'd prefer to be in the top three or four anyway. We thought this would be too bad because she seemed to have the right stuff. That next weekend had a shift open up on a Saturday morning that we needed to cover. We asked her, "Can you come in and work Saturday?" She came in, and she did great! We were thinking, *Saturdays are always good, but they're not that good. Something funny is going on here.* We thought perhaps it was a fluke. We asked her about it, and she said, "You know, I'm so glad you called me in because I really like the morning. I'm a morning person. I'm really awake in the morning. By the time I get to work here at five in the afternoon, I'm pooped. I just can't concentrate."

We never knew she was a morning person. You can't have a morning person working an evening shift after she is tired from the day; that doesn't work. So we moved her to mornings, and she did very well. Had we not known that we had her working in conflict to her body clock, we would have let a good employee go.

Here are some basic guidelines. You've heard these before, but they're worth knowing again: it's the person who makes the sale; it's the attitude that sells the customer. So hire someone who has a great attitude and has got spark and shine in her eyes. All of the duties can be trained, but you can't train someone to have fun dealing with people. That's just something they either have or they don't. So look for those kinds of people. Bring them in, test them, increase their responsibilities, and your sales culture will start to develop itself. As you bring in these talented people, they'll bring in their own stories and myths and legends and really help you build your sales culture.

Getting them into your sales culture is the first step. The next step is to keep them long enough to start increasing responsibility. The beginning stages of a recruit's career with you are significant. There are thresholds that people hit that you may or may not be aware of. There are several important thresholds that come up early on, particularly at two weeks, two months, and six months, when your employees are reevaluating their decision to stay. They ask themselves, *Did I make the right choice by coming on board here? Is this something I want to do? Am I doing the things I like? Am I getting what I need here?* These are times when you need to spend a few minutes with them, check in with them to find out what's happening in their minds. The very fact that you are checking in will give them an opportunity to voice concerns.

Keep the new people challenged because the worst thing you can do is let a talented and motivated person get bored. That's bad for two reasons. They will stop enjoying the newness of the position, and they will feel awkwardly underutilized.

Look at some of your current successes. Even if you have not been trying to build a sales culture, you have had successes in your business. Who's really doing well for you and why? You may not know who your most reliable performers are, or why they are reliable performers. Try to figure that out. It may be that you just got lucky and hired somebody with a great personality who is eager to learn and likes a challenge. Or maybe you did something, intentionally or unintentionally, to help develop them. So find out what it is you did to make these people be successful, and do that with the next group of people.

Start thinking today who your next good hire is going to be. I run into good retail people from time to time, and I take a note of where they work, who they are, and what their names are in case I have an opening and need to find them again. I sometimes carry a business card that says, "Thanks for being kind. If you are looking for another job, we are hiring sales and customer service people." You never know who you will run into. Not every position will be appropriate, but when you have a position that could be a good match, your recruiting efforts could be vastly simplified.

I have been asked before: if you find a potential employee, do you make room in the organization for that person or wait until an opening happens to approach that candidate? I'd say you have to answer that question in a couple of ways for yourself. This depends a lot on your management style. If you like to manage a week or two ahead of the wave or a week or two behind the wave, that's going to determine somewhat whether you bring the new person on board before you really need them or after you have an opening.

If you need to replace a weak player, then bring the new person on as a temporary. Give them some temporary assignments to make sure they're working out, and then allow the weaker person on the team to find new employment. That way you ensure you have a strong replacement before you let the weak employee go. But if everybody on your team is doing well, and you've found someone who you think is outstanding and you make room for that person, you've now increased your payroll costs. Can you justify it? Are you going to get enough value back in what that person's doing to justify the increase in your expenses? You may gain more benefits than you anticipated by bringing on a good new person. He or she may find many ways to bring value to your sales culture that you could not have planned. You have to ask yourself if the potential gain is worth the additional payroll.

One of the challenges in the self-storage business is that it can be somewhat seasonal. So there are times that we're hiring people, and there are times we're letting people go. Can you keep a good potential recruit waiting while you wait out the ebb and flow?

There certainly are challenges involved in hiring good people because it is true that good help is hard to find. And it is true that what we offer people is not for everyone, and you just have to realize that. Sometimes you have to let nice people go because the position you are trying to fit them into is just not right. You might feel bad about letting the person go. But it's not a good idea to keep them on and torture them, or to keep them on and let your revenues and customers suffer.

There is an interesting fact about wages. The money is not as important as you might think. I hear a lot of people at trade shows talk to each other, asking, "What do you pay *your* manager?" and "What do you pay *a* manager?" You have to pay people something. They have to make enough to make it worth getting up each day to go to work. They have to feel as though they are getting fair market value for the time, effort, and energy they put into growing your business. But do you know what? A dollar or two an hour doesn't make a bit of difference to someone if they're bored, if they're not challenged, or if they don't like what they're doing.

The main thing for people is to feel valued and to feel as if they bring value. If people like what they're doing, like the way you deal with them, and like the challenge involved in the job, a dollar or two an hour is not going to make a difference to them. So don't be so hung up on exactly what your wages are; be more hung up on how interested and engaged your employees are. Be more concerned about how much they enjoy their interaction with you, how well they take direction from you, and how well they give you feedback. Those are good indicators that tell you how your sales culture is coming together.

So now I challenge you to finish building your sales culture. Do something right now, in fact. Write down two things you are going to start implementing today to help build your sales culture. It's wonderful to read about methods or to go to seminars for tips and ideas. But if you don't implement them, then I am not sure I have brought you any value. I've enjoyed spending time writing about building a sales culture in any case, but I would like to run into you sometime and have you say, "Do you know what? Because of how you made me think, I did this and I did that, and here are the results I got. Thank you." That's what I'd like to hear if we have the opportunity to get together. So make a note: What are the two things you're going to do to move your sales culture forward?

Sales 101
StorageMart Pursued the Basics of Sales

Now that you are ready to move your sales culture in the right direction, you will need specific instruction on the art and science of sales. Some of this may seem like the same old speech on sales that you have heard before. Chances are you need to hear it again. If you are a golfer, you know that you need to always work on your game and review fundamentals. Why should sales be any different?

In this section I will present basic selling skills you can use no matter what you sell, no matter what you do, because you are always selling something— not just yourself, but your ideas, desires, products, and services. So Sales 101 should bring you some of the basic sales skills that successful salespeople use every day.

It is particularly important to review and relearn the basics of selling in the age of analytics and big data. If you believe what the technology sellers are saying, all you have to do to sell something to someone is to set up a *conversion funnel* and track the abandonment rates to see what converts and what doesn't. So much purchasing is done online that many people who are smart enough to know better are thinking that buying and selling are technical activities that are all about font size, button color, and click-through rates. Sorry to disappoint you, but only the technology and the ability to report on minutia have changed. People still buy things because they are emotionally driven to do so. They make their choices based on pain avoidance and pleasure attraction. They buy when it promises to bring them pleasure. They don't buy when something is a pain to acquire. CEOs and even heads of sales and marketing departments are tempted to believe that sales are all about the analytics and the data. The fact is that the reporting and the analytics only mean something if there is something to report or to analyze. The way to make things happen in business has not changed one iota. Things happen when someone sells something. Go back to the basics of selling, and your dashboard reports will start looking good. Funnel paths, abandon rates, and shopping-cart checkout ratios begin to acquire significance when there is good selling going on.

The first rule of selling is this: you can't sell anyone anything. You can, however, help people talk themselves into buying just about anything.

If this rule is true (read it again), then learning to sell is all about helping people talk themselves into buying from you. Okay, read on.

The first thing in sales is the *introduction*. Now, you hear some sort of an introduction anytime you walk into a store or make a phone call to a business: "Hello, how are you? How can I help you? Thanks for calling. My name is Joe. What can I do for you?" An introduction is important, but maybe not for the reason you might think. You might think it is important for branding or for telling the caller or visitor something about your differentiating factors. No. The reason the greeting is important is because a good greeting gives you a chance to smile with your prospect. Notice that I did not say, "smile at your prospect." Smile *with* your prospects. The power in a greeting is in a shared smile. You want people to hear and see you smile because they want a friendly exchange. They want to share a smile. Make it happen.

How many times have you gone into a store, and the retail person on the other end of the counter looked at you with a bored or even annoyed look and said, "Hello," and that was it? How much fun was that? How many times have you made a phone call to a business, and it was clear to you that you interrupted the person from whatever he or she was doing, and you got a frown, a gruff, or even a grump? How fun was that? No fun at all. What was your buying mood at that point? Close to zero, right? Let's not do that!

Smile. Say hello. Use your name if you want to; don't use your name if you don't want to. It doesn't matter. The whole point of the introduction is to share a smile with people immediately during their first seconds of being in your space.

A good smile breaks the ice, releases the tension, and tells your prospects that you are a real person who values their time, feelings, and money. Yes, all that happens in just one good smile. It does not matter what you say in your introduction, as long as it is not ridiculous or long-winded. Say it with a smile and mean the smile when you give it. An insincere smile is worse than none at all.

My rant earlier about big data and analytics prompts a question. How do you share a smile with a prospect who first finds you online? I can answer that for you, but I won't. If you build a sales culture and get all of your people smiling with customers, the answer will become self-evident. Let's get your people smiling first.

Now that you have a good greeting that will give your prospects a smile and put them in the mood to listen to you, let's get on with helping them talk themselves into buying from you.

The next thing you need to do in any kind of selling is to ask good discovery questions. Wait a minute, you say. Why are you asking questions? Shouldn't you be selling something? No! You can't sell people something by rattling at them, telling them this and that, and going on and on about stuff that probably doesn't mean anything to them anyway. That's not how you sell to people. That is certainly not how you help people talk themselves into buying from you. That's how you get people to walk out of your store, or, even worse, that's how you get them to close off their minds to you.

How you sell to people is to ask them good qualifying questions. For instance: Why did you pick up this book? What are you looking for in sales training? What techniques do you try that don't work for you? When have you been frustrated when trying to make a sale? Those are discovery questions.

So what you need to do is to find what questions work well for what you are selling. How many times have you walked into a clothing store, and the retail person asked, "Can I help you today?" That's not a qualifying question; that's an invitation for you to say, "No, I'm just looking, thanks," and shut off the whole process. How many times have you walked into a retail shop where the person has said to you, "Hi! Are you shopping for yourself, or are you looking for a gift for someone else today?"

How do you get away from that one? You can't just go, "Never mind. I'm just looking." It isn't that easy. You're now in a conversation. You have to say, "My mother-in-law has a birthday coming up, and I have no idea what to buy for her, and I'd better buy her something because she did something really nice for me a couple of weeks ago." Oh my gosh! Now the salesperson knows what you want and how to help you. That's why you ask good discovery questions. There is no other way to know how to help your prospects talk themselves into buying. So figure out what discovery questions work well for what you're selling, and then learn to listen.

How do you ask good qualifying questions on your website, Facebook page, or mobile app? I can answer that for you, too, but I won't. I will say this: I see lame attempts at this where a company is clearly separating people into demographics. Option paths such as "Click here if you are a business customer" or "Click here if you are a residential customer" cause people to choose a path and make a choice, but they are not selling questions. Once you develop a better sales culture and know which questions work in a live environment, you can translate those into web speak.

The best salespeople sell because they listen. If you listen, the prospects are going to tell you why they're interested in what you have to offer, why they're not interested in what you have to offer, and then you have someplace to go in your conversation. You have some way of knowing what the conversation is going to be. When you know how to listen, you will treat your analytics data as a means of listening, rather than a means of tracking. There is a huge difference between the two.

So ask your questions and listen. Hear what people are saying. People will give you buying signs. A buying sign is something like, "I was thinking about getting a Budweiser mug because I just love the Budweiser horse ads." My gosh! There's a buying sign for you.

Take that person to the beer mug section of the store and sell them a Budweiser mug.

Listen for buying signs!

Also listen for the person's concerns. The person might say, "I really would like a new suit, but you know, I just don't think I can get it this paycheck, unless I can find a real bargain." Well, okay. Now you know that if you can find this person something on the sale rack that's going to look like it didn't come off the sale rack, he can get it on this paycheck and not the next paycheck. You get credit for a sale today. The customer gets to look good now for less money than he had expected to spend. The store gets to clear out inventory and add revenue. Everyone wins! So listen to what the people are telling you.

During the discovery-question phase of your sales process, you also have the chance to raise important considerations. While you're listening to people talk, you're able to think about their situation and raise considerations that they normally would not have thought about. For instance, if someone is shopping for a self-storage unit to store Grandma's antiques, they might not know air-conditioned storage exists. Maybe they're scared to death to put that antique in storage because they don't want all of the joints to get out of whack. In your role as the storage professional, you explain that you have a climate-controlled unit in which the temperature will not get above 80 degrees, and the humidity stays under control. Now this person is thinking, *Oh, thank goodness! There's a solution for me.* Remember to raise important considerations for people. You know your business; they do not.

Your discovery questions will also allow you to qualify the prospect. Does the prospect qualify to buy this product? If you're selling a car, you need to know if your prospect has a driver's license. Does he know how to drive? Does he have money to buy the car? There are basic qualifications that you need to get past when you're trying to sell to anyone. In your discovery-question phase, you can find out: does this person have the means? Does this person have the authority? Is this sale going to happen if I can prove the value of the purchase and satisfy all of the concerns that might block the sale? Your discovery questions are important to determine not only if you have a genuine prospect in front of you, but to determine how this prospect will decide to buy.

Think how much fun a car dealer's website could be if it qualified people in this manner. If the "Do you know how to drive?" qualifying question linked to videos of people doing dumb things behind the wheel or people doing fancy driving moves, wouldn't prospects be in the right mood when they clicked the "Show me some cars that are available now" button?

What about if the "Do you have the money to buy a cool car?" question linked to videos of the world's most expensive cars and this dealer's most reasonable buys? What if there was a bar graph that showed monthly payments from $99 as a low to $1,500 as a high. When you moved the bar, the graph showed you what you could get for that amount of money. People would enjoy this interaction and convert at a much greater rate after clicking through to the cars they think they can afford. I am jumping ahead of myself by telling you how to get your website to sell. You need to get your people to sell first before you can even imagine how to get your technology to sell for you. You might think I am just avoiding the issue of how technology sells. But actually technology only sells when the people behind the technology know how to sell. This is true because the most effective web and mobile campaigns work when sales made over the phone and in person drive those campaigns.

Your discovery questions tell you where your prospect falls in your rule of thirds theory. Is this going to be a *gimme*? Is there no way a sale is going to happen any time soon? Is this a sale you are going to have to work for?

Your discovery questions are also going to allow you to build agreement with that person, and that's what selling is all about. No matter what you're selling, there are certain issues you have to agree on before the whole deal can come together, and the discovery questions help you build agreement.

For instance, if I were selling puppy dogs, one of the questions I might ask you is, "What breed do you like?" And if you don't want the breed I'm selling, uh-oh, we've got problems. There are basic issues in every sale that you have to build agreement on.

For instance, if you were renting a self-storage unit, when do you need that unit? If you don't need it soon, I'm not going to rent you one any time this month. If you don't know where my self-storage location is or how to get there, if it's not convenient for you to get to, we're not going to rent you a storage unit. Do you know what size you need? Can I help you figure a size? Do we actually have a size that is going to meet your needs? If we can't agree on these issues, I'm not going to rent you a storage unit. No matter what you're selling, there are certain issues you have to agree on. Find out what those issues are, build questions that will help you come to agreement on those issues, and go from there.

Pretend you're buying clothes at a retail shop. You need a new dress for Saturday night. What color do you like? What color do you think looks good on you? If we can't agree on the color of your dress, I'm not selling you a dress. What sort of a hemline do you like? Do you like a poufy skirt? Do you like it so it twirls when you spin? Do you like it tight? If we can't agree on these issues, I'm not selling you a dress. So find where you need to build agreement and come up with ways to do that.

Then create urgency.

Urgency means that the prospect you're selling to wants to buy now. It doesn't help you if that person buys later—although if you're selling products and services, you will need customers later—but you need customers now. So what is going to help that person buy now rather than later, or not at all, from you?

Why is it so important that the prospect buys now? Because when the mood to buy is high, resistance is low and attention is focused on making the purchase. The prospect wants to get this item marked off their to-do list. They see the purchase as a goal for their drive. Let the prospect satisfy that drive. If you let this window of high opportunity pass, then the prospect may get distracted and spend money elsewhere. The prospect may find another priority that trumps your offering. Or the mood to buy will subside, and the person's drive will be directed elsewhere. Just because a prospect expresses the intent to buy from you, that does not mean things won't change or other priorities might arise.

I have wanted a new electric guitar for about three years now. I have been in a guitar store at least six times. But I did not buy a guitar. Something always distracts me from my intended purchase. Someone in the store should have taken me off the market, but no one has yet. All someone has to do is to make some kind of suggestion to me. If someone in the store said, "That one looks like it fits in your hands pretty well," I'd buy. Give your prospect the satisfaction and peace of mind that an immediate purchase will bring. Give yourself the immediate revenue you need.

Let's take a look at what prospects need. Understand that purchasing from you now is a good thing for the prospect, whether or not the prospect expresses hesitation. What about that person who needs a dress on Saturday? If it's Monday, she needs to buy the dress now because she will need to make sure she can get the right shoes, the right hose, and the right accessories. If she waits until Thursday or Friday to buy that dress, and it doesn't fit quite right, she's in trouble. She needs to get the dress now so that she can get everything else in place by Saturday. If you let her walk out of the store without a dress, you are doing her a disservice. She will be stressed out the rest of the week worrying about the dress. And when she comes back, if she comes back, to your store on Thursday, maybe you will be sold out of her size or her color. Now you have set her up for a disaster. If you are in the fashion business, it is your job and your mission to prevent your customers and potential customers from experiencing a fashion disaster.

I am not joking. It is your job to prevent the fashion crisis. If you see every prospect walking into your dress shop as a person you can save from a fashion meltdown, be sure to give each customer an excellent fashion solution in plenty of time for whatever event is coming up. Every time you let a prospect walk out without a good fashion solution in her shopping bag, you have thrown someone to the fashion wolves to be mercilessly ravaged.

If someone is looking to rent a storage unit from your self-storage place, and it's your busy season, the prospect needs to rent from you now because you don't know what you're going to have available tomorrow. Whatever you're selling, you need to find a way to build urgency for that person. Limited availability, limited time, and limited opportunity—these are things that help people decide, "I'm going to buy now." If they think it's urgent, they will think they need to do something about the situation now. They need a nudge to say yes to the deal.

How do you, then, close the deal? Let's talk a little bit about the concept of closing. I don't know if you use the term the same way I use the term in selling. Closing a call, closing a deal, is not saying, "Thanks for coming by; hope you buy from us." That's not closing. Closing is getting the signature on the deal, on the contract. Getting the check, getting the payment: that's closing the deal.

Some people say using the word *close* sounds harsh. It sounds like someone might get hurt. I've heard it said that you should think about making a sale as if you were beginning a new friendship, opening a new account, or starting a new business relationship.

I still like the word *close* because it is the point where one relationship ends and another begins. This person is no longer your prospect after *the close*. She is now your customer or your client. So you are closing an old chapter in your relationship. You are no longer the potential vendor. You are now the vendor/consultant/expert of choice. You are also closing the conversation. There is no longer any need to discuss the black dress for Saturday night. Everything has been decided. You can now close the conversation and complete the transaction. The customer can close her internal discussion of the purchase. There is no longer any need to fret about Saturday. The outfit has been decided. All is well. It is time to devote thought and energy to something else.

So how do you close? You have to ask questions that lead you to the *big yes*. The big yes is, "Yes, I'll take this dress," "Yes, I'll rent that 10-by-10 storage unit," "Yes, I'll buy that puppy." That's the big yes you're leading to. Your discovery questions and your agreements help you get to yes because every time someone agrees with you on a small topic, a minor issue, or a simple concern, they're building to the big yes. Each time you and the prospect agree on something, fewer things will get in the way of his pending decision to buy now.

You should be constantly asking well-thought-out and pertinent questions that help close the sale all the way through the process. The most popular close that people use is the alternate choice; whether you know it or not, you've had it used on you a million times, and you've used it a million times. "Let's go to the movies. Do you want to go Saturday, or do you want to go Friday?" "Gee, I really like that outfit. Should I get it in brown, or should I get it in red?" You hear the alternate-choice close being used all day long. The first question a car salesman might ask you when you walk into the showroom is, "Would you like stick or would you like automatic?" The alternate-choice close rules all selling situations. It helps the prospect make decisions, which all lead to buying from you. It creates a decision tree the prospect can organize in his mind to go through all the options, small decisions, and minor considerations involved in making the big decision of buying now. So use the alternate choice whenever you can.

Figure out how you're going to do the alternate choice for your business. If you're burning CDs or DVDs for a living, ask if you should pack them in the jewel case or the paper case. Use your alternate choice. It works great.

Let's look at the concept called "closing on the minor issues." This is what building agreements is all about, and this is an easy way to build to the big yes. If I were selling you widgets, and I found out from you that you take five-hundred widgets a week, you like them on Tuesdays and Thursdays, you prefer them packed in grease rather than packed in bubble wrap ... by the time we get further down through our discussion, we've already agreed on every minor issue involved in the sale, and the only thing left for me to do is to hand you the pen and say, "Let me have your approval. I'll start you up next week." Every sale has many minor issues that can be resolved leading to the sale.

In self-storage, there are many minor issues as well. Will the new renter need a climate-controlled space? What sort of lock should your prospect choose? How will prospects get their belongings to the storage unit? Do they want to pay by check or credit card?

Look for minor issues involved in your product and service and figure out good ways to get agreement on each of them.

Another classic close is called the "puppy-dog close." I love it because I used to sell dogs. If I had a qualified prospect, and I knew they liked the breed I sold, they had a good environment for the dog, they had dog sense about them, and they knew how to handle a dog, I would not ask for payment. I would give them a dog well-suited for them, whether a puppy or an older dog, and say, "I'll tell you what, take the dog home. If in two weeks it's not working out, I'll be glad to just take the dog back." How many dogs do you think I took back again? Maybe one or two in a hundred. I had to take practically none of them back because I was careful about who I left the dog with and made sure the dog fit the situation.

The puppy dog close is so popular and effective they're doing it with cars now. How many of you have seen the overnight test drive? That is the classic puppy-dog close. The salesman says, "Here are the keys to the car. Bring it back tomorrow. If it doesn't work out, no problem." How many cars do you think they're selling this way? A ton! Do the car dealerships do a lot of prequalifying before they let you take the car home? You bet they do. This is how I bought my last car. The salesman, Jason, wouldn't let me give him back the keys. He said, after my overnight test drive, "If you need another day or two to get the financing approved, don't worry about it. Keep the car." I said, "It's Saturday. I am not going to get word back from my credit union until Monday at best." Jason said, "Don't worry about it. Enjoy the car for the weekend." Since I didn't force the keys on him and say, "I don't want the car," he knew he had a sale. I still like the car.

So if you can design a puppy-dog close with your product or service, do it! How many stores offer a simple return policy? You can buy clothes at just about any store, bring them home, wear them in front of the mirror, show them to your husband or wife, and if the clothes don't work out, you can take them back and get a full return on your purchase. It's a wonderful puppy-dog close. It is especial-ly effective when done on a credit card because no money changes hands until the purchase is confirmed. Find out how the puppy dog works for your situation and create one that works for you.

Another wonderful close is called the order-blank close. The the-ory behind the order-blank close is: if I'm filling out the order and getting all of your information . . . until you stop me we have a sale.

Have you ever been on the phone where the first thing the phone rep said was, "Can I please have your name . . . and a phone num-ber . . . and an address?" And pretty soon they've got everything they need from you to write up the order, and the only thing left for the telesales rep to do is to say, "Will you be using Visa, MasterCard, or

Discover today?" The order-blank close works wonderfully in self-storage, apartment rentals, and just about everything else. All you have to do is tell the person, "Let me just get a little information from you," and start filling out your lease or reservation forms. Use the order-blank close in your business. It is simple, low pressure, and easy for your staff to master.

I hope you find ways to apply all of these closes to your business. In order to learn what you need to know about each prospect and in order to use any of these closes, you will need to gather good information, which you do using well-phrased questions. You have read a lot about good questions in this book. Here are additional tips for building good questions.

Let's look at specific questioning techniques. There are a couple of kinds of questions you can ask; if you've studied sales before, you know what they are. I'm going to repeat them because they are worth repeating.

There are open-ended questions. Any question that's going to be answered by an explanation is an open-ended question. Ask as many of these as you can in the discovery phase and while you're building agreement because you want to know as much as possible, so you can know which way to take this prospect down the road to creating urgency and the close.

You're also going to ask closed-ended questions. These are questions that are answered yes or no. You need to ask these when you need specific information, when you need that prospect to make a clear decision about one option or another. It's a good idea to use a mix of open- and closed-ended questions. Just be careful which one you use and when you use them. If you use your closed-ended questions too soon in the process, the prospect may say no at a critical stage in the process, and you will have shot yourself in the foot. The closed-ended questions need to sound natural in the conversation, so do correct preparation before you use them.

Many times you can help people make decisions by paraphrasing what they just told you. Paraphrasing is an important technique to use whenever you're selling because it helps you to clarify what your prospect said. It also allows the prospect to hear what was said in your words, so he can confirm what was said to you. If you are completely lost, let's look at it from this point of view: I ask, "How soon are you going to need to buy that car? Do you have any events coming up where you'd like to look sharp in your new car?" And the prospect says, "I think I'd like to be in my new car by the end of the month," and I say, "Oh, so you think you'd like to be in your new car by the end of the month?" and the person says, "Yes." Now this person has committed to taking delivery by the end of the month. It will be difficult and awkward to tell me later that the car isn't needed until several months from now.

If your prospect says something, she may have been expressing her intent, or she may have just been thinking out loud. When you paraphrase and repeat the statement back to her, and she confirms it, then she has made a decision. It can no longer be just an act of thinking out loud or of talking to herself. There is no way this person can say, "I don't want the car until next month" because she told me she wanted it by the end of this month. I checked with her; she confirmed it. If she later says, "Oh, no, really I don't want it Monday. I really don't need it until Christmas," now she's stuck in a lie to herself. I need to sell her a car this month to make my numbers. I can hold her to that schedule if she told me once and then confirmed to me once more that this is her intention. Most people won't go back on something they confirmed to you.

If you use the paraphrasing technique to confirm information, that person is going to stick with what was said. If you're trying to sell someone on renting a self-storage unit, and he says, "I think a 10-by-10 unit will work for me," and you say, "Oh, so you think the 10-by-10 will work?" and he says, "Yes, it will," now he's in a 10-by-10.

Paraphrasing also works well to flush out the genuine issues that are preventing a sale from happening. If you ask the prospect to make the purchase, and the prospect gives you a reason why he is not ready to buy, try this: "If I understand you correctly, you feel that (whatever was said)." This allows the person to hear what he sounded like when he said it to you originally. Sometimes this will make the person think about what was said, and its importance will diminish. This is especially true when buying from you seems like a good idea. When your solution meets the prospect's needs, and the timing seems good, any reason to delay a buying decision might seem legitimate to the prospect when he says it. But when you say it back to that person, it might no longer sound like such a good reason, and you can more easily overcome the reason and still make the sale. These are just a few ways paraphrasing can work well for you. Notice that I paraphrased myself several times in writing about paraphrasing. I hope this helped drive the point home that something said once by your prospect may only be a test-sounding of the idea. But something said two or three times, or confirmed by your prospect when you asked for confirmation, becomes an intention.

When a prospect voices intention, a decision to purchase has been made. This is why your silence is often an important part of the selling process. You must learn to be silent. It's difficult because you're probably excited about what you're selling. You are excited about what you want. You want to get your way. You think you have one on the hook. You want to score a victory. People in sales like sales because they like the thrill of the fight and the ecstasy of the win; if you can't get the win, you don't like it. So you get excited about that. Sometimes you talk too much or talk too fast. Sometimes you know way too much about your product or service and want to share that information all at once.

You have to be quiet. Especially when you ask open-ended questions or when you're building agreement. You have to let the prospect talk because, as you know, in reality you can't sell anybody anything. You can only help people talk themselves into buying. They can't talk themselves into buying if all they hear is you going, "Blah, blah, blah, yada, yada." So they have to do the talking; they have to do the mental and emotional processing. You have to do the listening.

Yes, you have to keep control of the flow of the call or the conversation, how this sales process goes; if they can't talk themselves into doing it because they can't hear themselves think, the sale is not going to happen. You've got to be quiet. If you're selling on the telephone, there is a very simple technique to use: do a physical action that keeps you from talking. Bite your lip. Bite your knuckle. Do something to stop yourself from talking.

If you're talking in person with people, come up with a physical act you can do to stop yourself from talking. Tap your toe imperceptibly, pinch your finger, grab your leg, cross your fingers, or grip your pen (be careful how you do this, so you don't get caught). I was in an upper-management meeting listening intently and trying to hold my tongue. I have learned over the years to mostly hold my thoughts until the other people have finished speaking. This has not always been easy for me to do, so I try different bits of physical activity to make myself be quiet and listen carefully.

In that upper-management meeting, I was working a pencil in my hand. I was quietly and unobtrusively rolling it with my fingers and passing it between my fingers. While someone else was talking, I snapped the pencil in two—an embarrassing interruption! All I could do was to apologize and laugh at myself and let everyone else get some laughter out as well to smooth over the awkwardness of the moment.

I can't say enough about how much you have to work on ways to be quiet when it is time to be quiet.

Now that you are getting this far in the sales process that people are talking to themselves about whether to buy from you, you are going to hear reasons why people are not yet ready to buy. You will need to learn to deal with people's concerns.

You hear people talk about objections and rebuttals in the sales world. As I said in the last chapter, those are poor terms for what really happens. People don't object to what you're offering them. You don't have someone jump up and say, "I object to buying salsa with my chips!" That's not what they do. Buying is not a scene of two lawyers slugging it out in the courtroom, objecting to each other's lines of questioning. People are concerned that if they buy something, it's not going to work for them. They're concerned that they're spending money on something that's not going to work out. They're concerned that their friends might think they're idiots for spending the money on something goofy. They are concerned they will make a poor decision or that you will give them a bad experience. Figure out what concerns people have about your offer and how you can assure them that accepting your offer is a good move for them.

How you help people accept your offer is by understanding before you counter. If someone raises a concern, allow them to tell you what that concern is. You may have heard this concern fifty-seven times today, but if you cut that person off, thinking you know what they're saying, they're not going to like it. Let people finish what they have to say. Understand what they said. Read between the lines to understand their emotional positions. Use paraphrasing to help them to explain it some more, and then assure the person that what you are offering is a good thing. That's how it works. Understand before you counter; assure that person that their concern is not a new concern. Show them how your offering takes these concerns into account and makes everything better.

Try feel-felt-found (which I noted earlier). It's a wonderful tool that people use all of the time in selling. It is so good that it is worth repeating. Repetition is sometimes the best way to drive home an important sales feature and always a good way to internalize good sales phrasing. You may recall that the feel-felt-found goes like this: "I know how you feel. A lot of our very satisfied customers felt that way at one time too; what they found was that our solution was very well thought out and met their needs very well."

Use the feel-felt-found in just about every selling and customer-service situation. Feel with people what they're feeling. Let them know their feelings are legitimate. Let them know other people have felt that way. Maybe you even felt that way before coming to work for the company. Tell them what folks realized when they allowed the process to happen and did business with you. It works quite well, especially when you have some good, real-life stories on hand to illustrate the point. Here's where references and notes of recommendation, good reviews, and solid ratings can help a whole lot too.

Let's talk about how you know how to sell to the people you're selling to. Let's talk more about the rule of thirds. The rule of thirds assumes that one group of people who come to you are going to do business with you no matter what (unless you drive them off) because they've already decided what you have to offer is going to work for them. Another group of people is not going to do business with you now no matter what because their situation is going to change, they're not qualified, and maybe they don't have the ability or the authority. And a third group could go either way.

Now anyone who's halfway friendly and halfway knowledge-able will do business with the easy third. Sometimes you don't even have to be friendly or knowledgeable, you just have to know how to collect the payment. That's why fast-food companies make so much money with unskilled labor because when you're craving a taco, you're getting a taco no matter how untrained and unmotivated the people in the drive-through window or behind the counter are. That's what the fast-food companies bank on. They know that one group loves tacos and is coming for tacos no matter what. They invest their dollars in marketing, so the middle third that can go either way learns to crave their food. Your craving will make you buy, even in spite of less-than-good customer service and in spite of the fact that you really don't love tacos that much anyway. Creating a craving is the key to good marketing for most kinds of products.

Now, on the other hand, the people who aren't looking for tacos aren't even going to make the stop. So the taco makers don't care about that impossible third for immediate business. They do try to get the impossible third to reconsider their position with ad campaigns such as "Think Outside the Bun" or "Fourth Meal."

In every business, you make your money in that third that can go either way. These are the people who are targeted by advertising dollars. Those people who think they might want a taco only make the taco makers money when they actually buy the taco. If you know how to sell and how to ask your discovery questions and build agreement and create urgency and close the sale and help that person talk themselves into your offering, you're going to do business with a lot of people in that middle third. That's where you're going to make money.

Look at each and every sales opportunity with the rule of thirds in mind. "Is this person in the easy third? If he is, what can I do to make sure I don't chase him off? What can I do to make sure I let this sale come to completion?" If that person is in the impossible third, what can you do to give that person a good experience so when his situation changes, he thinks of you; then, what can you do to make sure those people in the middle third that can go either way start telling themselves that buying from you is looking like a good idea? Don't let them go somewhere else or decide they really don't want your product anyway. The middle third is where you make money, and how you make your money in the middle third is getting really good at Sales 101. Sales 101 brings results, and results, after all, are what we're all looking for.

Apply sales principles to every activity!

A Case Study: Since I do not know the particulars of your business, I am going to show you how the basic rules of selling can be applied to a basic and uncomplicated business. Let's apply a sales culture to self-storage. Using a basic consumer item such as a storage unit is a great way to test the sales culture theory you've been reading about. It is also a way to show you how a sales culture can be started, nurtured, and developed in any sort of business situation. If you think you have a sales culture in place already, this will help you see where you may have holes in your bucket. This is also a good exercise to see how a sales culture can transform an entire business class. As I stated earlier, it was the adoption of sales culture principles and practices that helped the self-storage industry compensate for a slowdown in new rentals and a pickup in the pace of move-outs during the dark days of 2007 through 2012. Had storage owners and operators not put sales culture principles into play, that industry might have been severely hit by this latest recession. If an industry as basic and uncomplicated as self-storage can see a quick and thorough turnaround driven by its adoption of a sales culture, then your specific business or your business class can benefit tremendously by going back to basic selling practices and applying them with gusto. In the next section we are going to pretend you run a self-storage business and are putting sales practices into place for the first time. Enjoy the exercise. Hopefully your internal dialogue will see many parallels to your current business and your creative juices will start flowing.

If You Were Building
a Self-Storage
Sales Culture

N ow that you have a clearer understanding of how to build your sales culture and the basic rules, methods, and theories of sales, let's talk specifically about using Sales 101 in a self-storage business. Let's pretend you own and operate a facility in a medium-sized market with six or seven hundred storage units. I am going to address you exactly as if you were in a seminar I conduct for storage business people, where I instruct them on how to create a sales culture and how to apply the basic Sales 101 principles in their businesses.

In this section we're going to study selling techniques and structures that work for selling self-storage and apply them directly to the situations you would find yourself in every day if you were in the self-storage business.

The first thing I'd like to cover with you is the challenge of operational changes. If you were a storage facility manager or an in-store storage consultant, and you're reading this, you'd have probably gotten this book from a regional manager, your operations director, or your owners, and you're thinking, *Oh, geez, not another training program. Oh, no, not another operational directive.* I feel for you. You have probably been given many operational changes to implement and many new sales directions to take. The follow-up from your superiors has not always been thorough. The strategies and initiatives have not always been well thought out either. You may feel someone is giving you grief by giving you this book, which represents yet another operational shift, and you're probably right. There is a certain amount of grief involved in adopting new ideas and implementing new programs.

If you are the owner, operations manager, or regional director I wrote about in the last paragraph, I apologize for suggesting that you hatch some half-baked schemes and then don't follow through on them very well. You often have too many irons in the fire, and even some of your sensible initiatives have died for lack of resources, attention, and follow-through.

The advantage that this book will hopefully give you is that you don't have to do anything but talk about it. If you talk about this book and the ideas, suggestions, and techniques I deal with, you will find yourself using some of them and taking a closer look at what you do and how you do it. This is all helpful to your business. Your staff, however, is probably grieving that you are now giving them more to think about, more to do, and new ways of looking at things.

I believe there are seven steps of grief that employees go through when experiencing operational changes. Typically, the first step is *confusion*. Your staff looks at you and thinks, *Oh, no, they're doing something else again. Ah, geez, what do they want from me?*

You can help them get through the confused stage by assuring them that you are trying to provide tools and skills that will help them better manage the business. You are trying to make their lives easier and more effective. This will help to reassure them.

Next they'll probably go through a *threatened* phase. Your staff is going to feel like, *Geez, do they think I'm not doing my job? What are they doing? Are they setting me up to get canned?* They will probably be threatened by the ideas in this book and the practices I am advocating. They are probably also thinking, *Hey, I've been doing this a long time. I know what I'm doing. You can't tell me how I should do things. I rent a lot of units. There are no new ideas.* New ideas and new practices always appear threatening at first.

You can help get your crew through the threatened phase by assuring them you would not invest in training and educating employees in whom you lacked confidence. Tell your crew about the successes people and companies have had implementing what I suggest. This will help them feel less threatened.

The next thing your people go through is a period of *resistance*. They're thinking, *What are they telling me I don't know already? I don't really need this.* They may tell you that the strategies and tactics I promote do not work. They may try something once and feel awkward about it and then tell you they will not try it again. But if you reassure people there is additional business to gain by learning and practicing what has been successful in other businesses and in other self-storage operations, they will go along with your experiment. At first they may go along just to humor you.

Then people go through the *tentative* phase. They will come to accept that some of these ideas might be worth trying. They will say something like this, "Okay, I'll try it. I'll read it. I'll listen to it. I'll put in the time. I'll give it a chance." I understand why they will act tentatively. I'd do the same thing if I were in their shoes and felt as if someone was giving me grief.

Then comes the *curious* phase. Your people will try a few things that work. Customers will respond in a positive manner. Your crew will begin to think, *Hmm, that's not a half-bad idea. Oh, well, that's one way of looking at things.*

The next thing you know, people will get excited. In this phase of *excitement*, your staff will begin to see successes and will want to try more new ways of doing and saying things. You may even become excited. You'll try one of my suggestions, and you'll go, "I'll be danged, it worked!" and you'll get excited and try something else and go, "Hey, that worked too!" And you'll sit down and look at some of the structures I'm going to give you and say, "You know, that halfway makes sense. That is how it works when you're selling self-storage." And you'll start working with this selling system, and you'll get into it, and you'll use it, day after day and with prospect after prospect, and you'll rent more units, and you're going to love it!

And then you'll experience *bliss*, and that's the place I want you to get to.

When all of this has been internalized and memorized, and you use it every day without really thinking about it, you will have totally forgotten about the day when people would slip away from you for no good reason. You will have forgotten how people used to stump you when they'd say, "I'm still shopping," "That's more than I'd like to spend," "I'm just shopping for prices," or "Oh, I can't rent today. I need to get permission from my husband (or wife)." All of those bad memories will be gone, and you'll be in self-storage bliss.

Yes, I'm halfway goofing around with you, but it is serious. This is how the process works when people are introduced to a new initiative and start working with it. They go through phases of resistance and acceptance that you have to help them through. You can't take a staff that has never used selling styles before and expect them to wake up the next day as dynamite salespeople. It is a process. You can't take people who have been given mixed messages by management, have been using mediocre sales techniques, have developed bad selling habits, or have never gotten training support to jump out of bed one day as master salespeople. It is a process. So let's get started selling self-storage.

What is the structure of the sales process in selling self-storage? Hopefully your store gets a lot of telephone inquiries; if so, much of your selling is done on the phone. But the same process holds true when someone walks in the door and asks, "How much is one of those storage things?"

We're not going to talk about dealing with current tenants now, so we're going to get them right off of the table. I am hoping that you and your staff already know how to be friendly and helpful to your current customers. If you learn to sell with better effectiveness, it will automatically improve your interactions with current customers. For the sake of keeping it simple, let's just talk about new potential renters.

The conversation will usually start one of two ways. It'll either be, "How much is—" and they'll name a unit they think they're supposed to get, or they'll say something like, "I need to store my stuff. Help me."

The people who start off asking for help are great to deal with. All you have to do is act the part of the storage expert, take them by the hand, and lead them through the process. The people who start out the conversation asking about price can sometimes be handled in exactly the same way, but sometimes they require more thorough and more careful handling.

Basically there are three things we're looking for in our sales structure. We're looking to build agreement with that caller because, if you recall from Sales 101, agreement is what this is about. We're also going to need an effective price stall, and what I mean by that is when someone asks you, "How much is that unit?" if you're not ready to tell them what the price is, you've got to stall that prospect, but you've got to stall them in a way that makes them comfortable. You can't just say, "Well, I don't want to tell you the price of that until I'm ready." That's not going to work.

There are also concerns people bring up when they're looking to rent a storage unit. The third part of the structure is dealing with concerns. The typical ones are: "I'm still shopping around," "That's more than I'm looking to spend," and "I need to get permission from somebody else before I can actually do this."

Let's first talk about building agreement with our prospect. I maintain there are only five issues you need agreement on before you can ask someone to rent from you. Let's look at those five agreements (check them off with your fingers). The first is time frame; if you can't agree with the caller that he needs the unit soon, you can't put one on hold for him. So the first qualifying question you ask is, "How soon are you going to need to store with us?" or "How soon are you going to need something?" "How soon?" If it's not until next year Christmas, your call is going to go quite differently than if he says, "I need it tomorrow."

The time-frame agreement goes on your thumb because if someone needs a unit right away, you've got a *thumb's up*. If someone needs a unit soon, that person will have tolerance for price and be willing to pay a little more. They will have tolerance for location and be willing to travel a little farther. They will have tolerance for features and amenities and accept pretty much whatever you have to offer. They will also have tolerance for size. They will accept a unit that is perhaps not exactly right for them because they do not have time to mess around. They need to get their stuff in storage soon.

The next agreement is the convenience of your location. "Do you know where we're located?" "Have you ever been by here?" "Do you know where we are on 5th Street?" That's an important question to ask because if the caller or the prospect knows where you're located and says, "Yes, it's a convenient location," you're halfway home. The reason people store someplace is because it's convenient for them to get to. Location is the number one reason people rent. So agreement number two is the convenience of the location.

Location goes on your index finger because it is the number one reason people select a storage place. If your location is convenient for your prospect, that prospect will have tolerance for everything else.

Size is the next thing you have to agree on, and most people who've been in the storage business for more than a few minutes are great at helping people figure size, but here are a couple of things to consider: it's not important what size *you* think they should fit in; it's important what size *the callers* think they should fit in. And it doesn't matter what you agree on as long as it's close. If that person really needs a 10-by-15, but she agrees she needs a 10-by-10, you're going to show her a 10-by-10 and a 10-by-15 when she comes down anyway. Now if she needs a 5-by-5, and you agree she needs a 10-by-20, that's a different story, but as long as you're close, it doesn't matter. I once made a secret shop to a storage facility where the manager argued with me for five minutes over what size I needed. What a waste. "Mr. Caller, it sounds like you might fit in a 10-by-10 or maybe a 10-by-15. If you can visualize your belongings in one of those sizes, which one do you think might work best for you?" The caller says, "Hmm, probably the 10-by-15." Great! Hold a 10-by-15. Show a couple of other sizes when the person comes down just to make sure he has what he needs.

Size is the third agreement, and it goes on your middle finger. It goes on your middle finger because size does matter, but only in helping you build the alternate-choice question. It also goes on your middle finger because if you give size too much focus and let it be the main thing you focus on, it is like sticking your middle finger up all by itself, and that could get you into all kinds of trouble. So don't focus too much on size. Just use it to offer a good alternate choice close on the size agreement.

Agreement number four is amenities or features. The other reason people select one storage place over another is because they like the security and the convenience features. So find the best features of your property that have to do with security and convenience and build phrasing and questions that will allow you to reach agreement on amenities. "What's great about our store is that we've got an access-control gate so that only tenants can come and go with their PIN code, and we're well-fenced and well-lit. So you can tell we take security very seriously here, and after all, isn't that what you're looking for in storage? Plus our store is really convenient to use because one of the great things we have is a covered unloading dock so that you can pull in out of the sun and out of the rain and unload and load your belongings. What's neater than that?" And the caller says, "That is really neat." Now you've got an agreement on convenience and security features.

Your features and amenities build value into your offering. Most people think one storage place is pretty much like the next and that all they are renting is dead air to fill up, but that is not all they are getting. They are getting the peace of mind in knowing their goods are safe and secure. They are paying for the conveniences you offer. They are paying for the security and the perceived security. They are paying for great customer service. They are paying for things they wouldn't even know about if you did not tell them. When people agree that you have built a good offering with good features and amenities, it is easier for them to justify paying the rent.

Features and amenities go on your ring finger because if your prospect agrees you have a good place to store, it is like she has become engaged to you to be your next customer. Agreement on amenities is like an engagement ring!

Price is the fifth agreement. Price goes on your pinky finger. Prospects have to agree that your price is reasonable; that they're prepared to pay that price. They don't have to agree they like the price. Most times a caller has no idea what storage is all about, and he thinks that price is the most important consideration. Price is not the most important consideration. Everyone wants to know their money is well spent, but most people are concerned with convenience *and* value. So until you've had a chance to reach an agreement on the convenience of the location and on the amenities, that caller doesn't know what your unit is worth. You've got to make sure he or she knows that value. "A 10-by-10 is worth $100 because you have (this amenity and that amenity and the other amenity)." So price is the fifth agreement.

Price goes on your pinky finger because, even though it is an important consideration, price is much smaller than you might think.

How do you get through the first four agreements before giving the price? Let's look at the concept of the price stall. The first words out of that caller's mouth might be, "How much is a 10-by-10?" You think you need to respond directly to the question. But think about this for a minute. If you give the price right away, then you are enforcing the prospect's notion that price is the main issue. Bad idea. People often lead with the price question because they don't know what else to say, or because they erroneously think price should be the main consideration. Well here are a couple of things you can say to get the chance to go through a few agreements before you give them a price.

Price stall number one: "Let me pull up my price screen, and while that's loading, let me tell you a little bit about us. Now how soon did you say you were going to need something? Oh, okay, great! And do you know where we're located over on 5th Street? Okay, well then you know we're a really great place to store because we have this convenience and that convenience. Sounds like it's a convenient place to store, doesn't it? And we also have this security feature and that security feature, which means we take security very seriously. And after all, you do too, don't you?"

Wow! Before you know it, you already have three agreements out of the way. You haven't even talked about size or the price, and the caller is perfectly fine with it because your price screen is loading. Now up comes your price screen. You can talk about size, figure out price, and set a time to get the caller in the store. Few people will argue with this price stall because they do not assume you know every price off the top of your head. They understand that it takes a minute to load a computer screen, if you explain that you have many sized units and pricing changes often, so you cannot keep all the prices in your head. You also might need to add that your internet is running a little slow, if that is the case. Most point of sale or retail management operating systems are web based. The staff people are at the mercy of bandwidth speed . Consumers are very savvy. If you don't explain why you need to see your price screen, or why it takes a minute for your price screen to load, they might assume you are using a price stall just to stall them...and then your price stall backfires and your potential renter has become annoyed and frustrated with you. When you explain your situation, this price stall is perfectly natural, if in fact you do not know all the prices off the top of your head and your internet speed is a bit dragging. If you don't explain your situation, or if you are lying about it, you will embarrass yourself and probably lose the customer.

You may have many issues like this in your business. Consumers do not mind being delayed or having minor inconveniences if they know that there is a good reason. If they don't know the reason or don't believe the reason to be true because of some subsequent information, you are sunk.

Price stall number two: "In order for me to quote the right price, let me just ask you a few questions." That's hard for someone to say no to. They're not going to say, "No, just tell me the wrong price." They're going to let you ask them a few questions, and so you start: "Tell me how soon you're going to need something. Do you know where we're located, and is that a good location for you? This is a great place to store because we have this feature, which means . . . and that feature, which means—" and now before you've given the price, you've gotten several agreements out of the way.

Price stall number three: "A lot goes into the price of a storage unit. Let me tell you what your money buys you here." Now we're starting to build a value proposition right from the beginning. This person is not going to interrupt you because you've already offered a value challenge. The caller will want to hear why your place is worth it. So now you've got a chance to build agreement before you go to price. Using this price stall means you begin by bragging on your property's features, reach agreement on features, and then move into your time frame and location agreements.

Price stall number four: "Since availability affects pricing, tell me how soon you're going to need a unit, and I'll see what's available." Now you're doing all kinds of things. You're getting permission to get more information, you're building urgency right away, and you're letting the caller know that it's just not always that easy to get a storage unit.

The easiest price stall is to just ignore the price question and say, "Sure, I can help you with that; how soon are you going to need your unit?" and go right into your qualifying questions. Few people will protest with this approach; it is easy to master and easy to say.

Let's review these price stalls because you've got to use them verbatim until you really learn them. Don't just try them in your own words to begin with, or you'll end up saying something like, "Let me pull on my price, and while I'm loaded, tell me something!" You can imagine the kind of reaction you might get to that.

It just won't work to put these price stalls in your own words right away. Let me repeat them so you can see them again. "Let me pull up my price screen, and while that's loading, let me tell you a little bit about us." "In order for me to quote you the right price, let me just ask you a few questions." "A lot goes into the price of a storage unit, and let me tell you what you get for your money here." "Since availability affects pricing, tell me how soon you're going to need a unit, and I'll see what I have available." "Sure I can help you with that; how soon will you need your unit?"

This is how you allow the caller to allow you to build agreement; to let you build some value before you give price. Most people have no idea what a storage unit costs, and cost should be the last thing you discuss whenever possible. Whether it costs a dollar or a hundred dollars, it costs more than storing in their uncle's attic for free, and that makes it seem expensive to first-time storage customers.

You also have to understand that storage buyers have a language all their own. You have to understand that it is a foreign language. "How much is a 10-by-10?" when translated into English actually means, "Please tell me why I should store with you." If you understand this, then you will be able to effectively use the price stalls. But you do have to use them like scripting.

The reason they call specific sales phrases a "script" is because you must use the phrases verbatim. When you see a theatrical play, the actors use the script as written. There are certainly revisions in rehearsals, and there are rewrites after audiences have reacted or not reacted as the author had intended. The actors say the lines as written because the lines have been carefully crafted to bring a certain reaction from the audience, to give the audience a certain impression, or to cause the audience to think in a certain way.

This is also why it is difficult for some people to tell jokes. If they do not tell it just right or do not deliver the punch line exactly as intended, the joke falls flat or bombs all together.

When you have mastered these phrases and know how to get the right reaction from prospects, cause them to think the right sorts of things, and paint the right pictures in their imaginations, then you can put these phrases in your own words to suit your personal style or to suit the person you are talking to.

Improvising sales phrases before you know how to use them is like letting someone go target shooting in the woods with a pistol before he or she knows how to handle the pistol in a controlled environment such as a shooting range.

Mishandling sales phraseology may not hurt you physically, but you can easily shoot yourself in the foot figuratively. You can cause real damage if you do not master sales phrases before you try to use them as you see fit. You can chase off a prospect, cause a customer to quit doing business with you, or fool yourself into thinking that sales phrases do not work. Chasing off customers and prospects causes real damage to your revenue and to the reputation of your business, both of which need to exhibit positive growth in order for you to prosper over time.

Now here's my disclaimer on price stalls: sometimes you have to give the price too early because someone says, "Give me the price on a 10-by-10," and while you attempt to build agreement by saying, "Oh, great, tell me how soon you're going to need something," he says, "Just give me the price of a 10-by-10." Well, okay, now you have to take a different tack, and here's how you handle that one: "That 10-by-10 is only $98, and here's what $98 buys you at our store. At our store we have this feature, which means . . . and this feature, which means—"

Whoa! Now before you know it, you're building agreement. You've given the price as the customer demanded, but you haven't given the prospect a chance to say something like, "That's more than I'd like to spend" or "I can save five bucks down the road." You cannot pause between the price and the "here's what it buys you" phrase. If you pause, you will lose. The prospect will think you have said all you have to say, and he or she will likely end the conversation. Or the prospect will take control of the conversation, and you will not be able to regain it. If you do not pause, you will be able to build agreement at the same time as you've taken price out of the picture. This is not a response for the weak or the inexperienced. You need to do this one with confidence and authority, or it will not work.

If you do not use confidence and authority in your voice while giving the price too early, the prospect will think he or she has you intimidated, and the sales process with this prospect will be difficult to guide and unpredictable in its outcome.

If you have to give price too early, "That 10-by-10 is only $98, and here's what $98 buys you at our store—," you need to focus hard on keeping the rest of the conversation on track and getting agreement on time frame, location, amenities, and size.

There is more importance in the price stall than just being able to build value before talking about price. At some point during the first two or three qualifying questions, you're going to find out whether this person lies in the easy third—do you remember your rule of thirds?—or whether that person is in the impossible third, or whether that person is in the third you're going to have to work for. If someone calls you up and says, "How much is a 10-by-10?" and you say, "Since availability affects pricing, let me find out how soon you're going to need it, and I'll see what I have available" and the caller says, "I talked to my uncle Joe. He stores with you. He's going to help me move in on Saturday." You don't need to worry about this one. This is an easy third. Just don't blow this one by talking too much, and you're going to be fine.

You're going to get somebody else who's going say, "How much is one of those storage garage things?" And you say, "How soon are you going to need something?" and the caller says, "I won't need it for four years when I will retire"—that's going to be a whole different call.

And then you'll get the ones in the middle you're going to have to work for, and here's where you'll have to get good at dealing with concerns. The biggest concern normally is the *not ready*. You've gone through your agreements, you feel like you've gotten somewhere with this caller, and you attempt to put a hold on that unit. First of all, how do you attempt to put a hold on that unit? You do that by creating urgency with limited availability. "It sounds like you're going to fit into that 10-by-10. Does that sound like a good unit to you?" "Yes, it does." "Great. Since availability is limited, the best way I could help you today would be to put that unit on hold for you. What's your first name?" And you begin your order-blank close. Before you get very far, the prospect says, "Wait a minute; I'm not ready to rent anything yet."

Okay. What does *not ready* mean? Does it mean he is not ready to store or not ready to store with you? So ask a few questions. "Are you moving, or do you just need to get a few things out of the way?" "Have you called a few places yet? What did you find?" Find out what's going on with their situation. At some point, he'll say, "Really what the issue is . . . I don't know when my house is going to close. I haven't even called the real estate agent yet. I don't know what I need," and you find out the real story. Now you can help the prospect realize it would be best to get the storage unit now and be able to stage the house for quicker sale and start getting organized for the move.

Or the prospect may say, "I talked to XYZ Storage down the street, and they're five dollars cheaper than you." Now you have someplace to go with the conversation because you can explain how the value of your place is worth way more than five dollars, and storing with you is the best way to go.

The other concern people will bring up when you say, "Since availability is limited, the best way I could help you today would be to go ahead and put a hold on that 5-by-5. What's your first name? And your last name? And your phone number?" is often, "Oh, no, I'm still shopping." What does that mean? Sometimes it's just a stall that has nothing to do with shopping, so ask them a few questions: "Have you called a few other places yet? What did you find?" If they are shopping, are they shopping for price? Location? Size? Amenities? Are they shopping for a good customer service experience? Go back to your agreements; see what's going on.

If they're determined to call other storage places for units first, try this: "Let me give you a few things to look for." Now you're setting the standard. Any other place they call is going to be compared with your store because you're giving them what they should be looking for. "Let me give you a few things to look for. You should have a facility that has—" and then go through your list of amenities because if someone else doesn't have those, the customer shouldn't be storing with them. Or try, "Have you called a few other places yet?" You'll hear what that person has to say. They may say, "We like your price a lot, but we don't like your location," or "We like your location, but we don't like your price." Find out what their concerns are so that you can understand them.

Another thing you can try is to say, "So that I have a better idea on how we might be able to meet your needs, tell me a little more about your priorities." Wow! Now you're going to get a whole story from that person. It's a tricky phrase that's not easy to digest. Let's try it again: "So that I can have a better idea on how we might be able to meet your needs, tell me a little more about your priorities." If you can get good information from people using this phrase, it'll help you build value, differentiate your store from the next store, and help the prospects talk themselves into spending ten dollars extra to store with you, where they'll be a lot happier.

The other concern you get is, "I have to ask my spouse first." This is normally just a bunch of wallow willows because those who are storing something have already talked to their spouse about it. They're not just calling out of the blue unless you're dealing with a marriage breakup. That's another story entirely, and people in a marriage breakup certainly don't need spousal permission to get a storage unit. "I need to talk to my spouse first" is often just an attempt to fake you out. Here are a few ways to find out if it's true or if someone is trying to put a move on you to dodge a decision. Ask the prospect, "Have the two of you already talked about storing?" Oh! "And have you decided what you're going to store? And have you decided when you're going to need to store?" If they have already talked about it, then the risk to them of getting in trouble with their spouse by reserving a storage unit with you is next to nothing. The risk to them is making the phone call and not reserving the unit because if that person has already discussed all of this with a spouse, he or she will not get a good response at home if there has been no reservation or no rental. If spouse A goes home and says, "Honey, I called the storage place; it sounded great," spouse B is going to say, "Did you get a unit?" and spouse A will say, "No," and spouse B will say, "Why not? What are you waiting for? Can't I trust you to get anything done?" You can save your prospects from having this conversation if you help them decide to rent now or at least to reserve a unit.

So let's talk realistically about how these partnerships work. If they've already talked about storing, then the best way you could help them would be to take the hassle out of this situation and reserve a unit for them: "If you've already talked about storing, and you've already pretty much decided what you're storing, wouldn't your wife (husband, partner) be pleased if you went home later and said, 'Honey, I have it all taken care of. One less thing we've got to worry about. They'll have the unit ready for us Saturday.'" Now he or she goes home a hero. This works great most of the time. If somebody says, "I have to ask my wife," "I have to ask my husband," or "I have to ask my partner," use the three-question response. It will not work every time. But even when it does not work, it is still a great setup for inviting both partners down to the store to look around and select a unit they can agree on. Setting an appointment for both spouses to take a quick tour is never a bad secondary outcome of the conversation.

In the worst case scenario, you can tell the spouse you are talking with all the reasons why the other spouse will like storing with you, so he or she can be your proxy salesperson and close the deal for you. This will work especially well if your proxy salesperson can create urgency for you.

Let's take another look at building urgency. We dealt with this earlier; this is so important because people love to procrastinate when it comes to spending money on things other than what they love to spend money on. "Limited availability" is the key phrase because the fact is you never know who's going to rent something from you tomorrow; particularly in the busier eight months of the season, someone could rent you out of a 10-by-10 fast. So limited availability is a true condition.

You want people to get in their units now so they can start moving in slowly, so they don't have a big crisis when it comes down to zero hour on moving day. Use your limited availability to help those people get in sooner. It goes like this: "Since availability is limited, the best way I could help you would be to go ahead and put a hold on that unit for you. Now what was your first name?" and go to your order-blank close. This simple phrase is how you put a hold on the unit for people.

It is your job to prevent someone from having a storage crisis. If you actually worked at a storage property, you would have certainly had people show up at five minutes to closing time in a moving truck looking like a sweaty, dirty, frustrated mess. And they need a storage unit right away. You also have had people who talked to you last month show up at the store only to find out the unit they wanted is sold out, or the special they wanted to take advantage of is finished. Do not let this happen. Keep people from having a storage crisis by getting them in their units now.

What I have hopefully given you in this section is a way—a structure, a few specific sets of techniques—to take that call from "Hello" to "When do you need it?" to "Oh, I understand your concern, but here's why our place is a great place to store" to "Let me hold that unit for you; I'll see you Saturday" to "Here's your receipt, and thank you for storing with us." This is an intentional process you need to learn, just as you might learn any other process. Work on it, and you will see excellent results.

How did it feel to read this section? Were you able to pretend to be in the storage business? Did you find a structure that would allow you to handle a storage inquiry? Did you find you were able to draw parallels with your actual situation? Did you find yourself thinking of similar situations in your own business? Did you see yourself taking one of these techniques or phrases and molding them to your industry?

Get Inside Your
Customer's Mind

Now that you are becoming engrossed in the sales culture discussions, let's take the subject one level deeper. It really doesn't matter what you do, as long as you know that it will satisfy your customers. How do you know you are doing it right? You have to get inside your customer's mind to understand the emotional background and the internal dialogue your customer experiences.

There are plenty of places to rent tools and equipment in Columbia, Missouri, where I live. If I need to rent a power tool or garden implement, I go to Lindsey Rentals. It is not a sparkling clean place: it looks kind of like a big tool shed, with all the grease and dust you might expect. But it is a fun place to rent because the owners and staff know their customers, if not by name, then by face. And when they recognize you, they tell you off-color jokes, give you grief, tease you, and otherwise give you a hard time. As the customer, you are expected to tease them back, give them a hard time, and share a few laughs. It is fun just to stand there and watch the exchanges between the staff and the regular customers, especially the commercial and construction customers. It is a wonderful way to run this type of business. It also seems to be a great way to get your regular customers coming back for more. Can you imagine the potential loss of income if someone who regularly rents a backhoe for $600 a day goes to rent somewhere else?

I have no idea if their prices are higher or lower than anyone else's. I don't care. What I know is this: spending time and money to do projects around the house may be enjoyable at times, but most projects are not pleasurable; they are a chore. Spending money to rent a piece of equipment is painful. Spending time to get the equipment is a pain in the neck. Most people who rent equipment are guys. What makes us come back to this tool rental place is the pleasure we get from poking fun at the owner and getting picked on in return. Sherman and Billy, who own Lindsey Rentals, have by accident or by design found a way to balance out the displeasure and discomfort involved in renting tools and turn the whole experience into a pleasurable one.

I bought a used lawn mower from them recently. I have learned that people leave their mowers for Sherman and Billy to repair and then abandon them. Being the thrifty person I am, I discovered I could buy a $200 mower for $60 this way. I took my bargain home and the darn thing stalled out. I took it back to Sherman and Billy and left it with them for a few days. It seemed to have some dirt in it that was making it stall, and it didn't take much for them to get it ready to mow. I took it home, and it ran fine for a few minutes. Then it died. Drat! Of course I was disappointed. I took it back to Sherman at about half an hour to closing time on Sunday afternoon. Sherman stopped what he was doing and opened up the mower to flush out whatever dirt was missed the first time. He didn't have to, but he did. He could have let it wait until his mower technician came in on Monday. But rather than complaining about having to take my mower back a second time for a simple fix, I am telling you about the awesome customer service at Lindsey Rentals. A potentially big pain turned into a simple and unexpected pleasure.

We all have our own shopping styles and preferences. No matter how you slice it, shopping and buying comes down to basic pain and pleasure stimuli and response. We are subject to conditioning. Places and actions that we associate with pleasure we seek to experience again. Experiences that cause us pain we seek to avoid. Your customers go through this process during every contact they have with you.

Do a simple experiment. Make two columns on a piece of paper. Title one "Pain" and title the other "Pleasure." Then walk through the entire process your customer walks through while dealing with you. Make a tick mark each time you think something causes pleasure and one each time you think pain is the result. You may be surprised at the number of tick marks on the pain side.

How much pleasure or pain does your customer expect? Expectation is the filter through which your customer views and internalizes the pain and pleasure of dealing with you. An expected pain does not hurt as much or last as long as an unexpected one. An expected pleasure does not feel as good or last as long as an unexpected one.

What pains are unavoidable or common to all suppliers of your service? What pains are unique to your operation? What pleasures are common to the shopping experience your customer could have at any of your competitors? What pleasures are unique to your operation? The answers to these questions differentiate you from your competition for better or worse.

Let's drill it down just a little further. What pleasures offset which pains? Which pains offset which pleasures? If a pain is not offset by some sort of pleasure, then the pain does not go away. In the same vein, a corresponding pain can erase a nice pleasure.

Let's extend our case study in your fictitious storage business. What is a typical storage experience like? If you don't know, I'll tell you.

Joe and Edna are building a new house. There are all sorts of pains and pleasures involved here. Hopefully, the expected pleasure of having a dream home will sustain them through the process. But their existing home sells more quickly than they expect for the asking price. There is pleasure in knowing they got what they wanted for the house and that they will not be carrying two mortgages.

However, the new house isn't ready, and they will have to live with Edna's parents until the new house is ready. Major pain here. Their entire household will have to go into storage. That means they will have to move twice. That means they will be living away from the things they hold dear. Their routines will be interrupted for months. They will have to deal with Edna's parents. Joe and Edna need counseling and a week at a spa more than they need storage, but they stop by your property because Edna passes it on the way to work. This could be pleasure. She is going into a place she is familiar with because she sees it every day. Hopefully, your curb appeal is nice, and this causes her pleasure.

How does it go from here? Is it a pain or a pleasure to deal with your store staff? Is it pain or pleasure to select a unit, sign the lease, and put a lock on your unit? Are the painful parts of the process offset by simple pleasures?

You would run an audit on empty units and on cash transactions if you had a real storage business. Why not run an audit on the customer's experience? Mark each transaction, impression, and experience as: 1) expected pain; 2) unexpected pain; 3) expected pleasure; 4) unexpected pleasure. If a pain is cancelled out by a pleasure, indicate that. If a pleasure is cancelled out by a pain, indicate that too.

Now you have a framework from which you can begin to manage the experience your customer has while dealing with you.

Roller-coaster operators, toymakers, and restaurant developers have been managing the experiences of their customers forever. Use some of these questions to determine your next course of action. What pains can be avoided? Which pains can be minimized? Which pains can be offset by a corresponding pleasure? Which pleasures can be enhanced? Which pleasures are so fun or so unexpected that they set the tone for the whole experience?

Remember the self-storage operator who has a fresh batch of chocolate chip cookies at the counter at all times? He thinks the cookies allow him lots of room to make mistakes in handling customers because everyone loves the cookies.

Sherman and Billy at Lindsey Rentals don't need to do anything better than their competitors. They can even get away with doing a few things worse. They can get away with causing a few unexpected pains because the pleasure of having a belly laugh when you hear Sherman insult one of his best customers is worth the time and expense of driving to his shop and renting something.

I'm not suggesting you have a "Your momma's so ugly—" contest with your customers, or that you bank your operation on the tollhouse chocolate chip recipe. But you do need to find something fun and pleasant in your transactions. It may be as simple as having a pleasant atmosphere in your office, having your store manager step out from behind the counter to greet people in a retail environment, or having a quick check-in process at your restaurant.

If you don't do something to audit your customers' experiences, you leave too much to chance. This will go a long way in determining what is going on inside your customer's mind.

Let's extend our case study once more to see how getting inside your customer's mind would have a real impact, even if your business was that six- or seven-hundred unit storage property in Anytown, North America.

The First Rule of Selling

The question that potential self-storage renters ask themselves is: "To rent or not to rent?" Many times, we think that our customer is a mysterious animal. Not so. I'm going to take you on a trip inside the mind of our storage prospects and customers. We are going there so you will know how to help them talk themselves into "buying" a storage unit. After running this exercise for your make-believe self storage enterprise, you should be ready to get in tune with the internal dialogues of your real-world prospects and customers so you can help them talk themselves into buying from you.

Most people who need a storage unit are not at a happy time in their life. Even if they're getting a storage unit because they just got their dream job in their dream city, and they're going to be making three times the money they were, and they will be living by the beach, they still have to move. Have you moved recently? Would you rather cut off a toe than move again? Unless professional packers and movers do the entire process while you are on vacation, moving is not a joy.

After we moved the last time, I promised my wife the next time we move, I'm just taking my toothbrush; I'm leaving everything else behind. We'll have the auction people come in, clear it out, and we'll start over. Now that we've been in the house a few years, I think the next time we move, I'm not even taking my toothbrush. The moving process is not a pleasant experience. The whole process of settling in after a move also takes a lot of energy.

Many people over the last few years have needed storage because of misfortune, foreclosure, downsizing, layoffs, adult children coming home, elderly parents passing on, and many other life-changing events. Some people have chosen storage as a lifestyle choice to help them manage their belongings, to save things for future generations, or to get *feng shui* in their homes. Unless you know if the situation that created the need for storage was a happy or an unhappy one, you do not know what to do next.

Let's assume that self-storage is a selling game. This means you are selling to people who are often not in the best frame of mind. You know my first rule of selling: you can't sell anyone anything. All you can really do is help people talk themselves into buying from you. In other words, you sell things to people not by selling to them, but by helping them sell themselves. Now that's kind of a roundabout way of getting to the sale, but how you shorten that course is with a technique, a tool, a way of thinking called "assuming the sale."

It's a simple game that you play with yourself. You assume that every person you talk to is going to buy from you. This is not just a simple bit of positive thinking. It is a powerful tool, a powerful stance. If you believe that every person you talk to is your next renter, then you will treat them like your next renter. Since people act the way they are treated, they will act like your next renter. When you treat them like a renter, then they have to talk you out of the rental, rather than you talking them into the rental. If you take that approach with people, you will have the kind of confidence in your property, in your presentation, in yourself that will become infectious. When have you dealt with salespeople who were sure you were going to do business with them? How difficult is it to say no to that kind of a person? It's difficult because you know you're talking to them because you had some kind of an interest and because you would really like to get the issue off of your mind and off of your to-do list. You don't walk up to the greeter at a restaurant and hear that person say, "Gosh, do you think you might want to eat with us tonight?" The greeter really says, "How many? Smoking or non-?" and takes you to your table. That's the same approach you should take with people you're dealing with. If you go away with nothing else from this read, learn to play a trick on your own mind to assume that everyone's going to buy from you. That change of attitude alone will boost your business immediately.

Assuming everyone who presents themselves as a prospect is your new customer is only the first step.

The next step is to get inside your prospects' minds. I don't mean you should read their minds. I mean you have to influence their emotional and rational processes in order to help them talk themselves into doing business with you. The trick to getting inside the minds of your prospects is to learn their internal dialogue. People have an internal dialogue going much of the time. As you're talking to your prospects, they're talking to themselves. And you're also talking to yourself at the same time. While you are vocalizing, "Sure I can help you with that," you may be thinking to yourself, "Gosh, I hope this person rents from me. I've got one 10-by-20 left. I hope I can rent it today." You might also be having an internal dialogue about things completely unrelated to what your vocalized thoughts are. You might be vocalizing, "We take Visa, MasterCard, or Discover," but your internal dialogue is going. "Geez, I hope the kids got off to school okay today." You've got all kinds of things running through your head when you're talking to people, and they have all kinds of things running through their heads at the same time. So if you can say to yourself, "I'm going to rent to these people," now you're assuming the sale, and it becomes the power you need to make the sale. At the same time, your job is to influence or at least to understand the internal dialogue of your potential customer.

The internal dialogue phenomenon is happening right now. You're talking to yourself right now while you're reading this. You may be processing what you are reading, and at the same time you might be thinking, *Gosh, what's this Tron guy doing? I stayed up too late. I hope my 401K increases in value this quarter. Why is Tron going on and on about internal dialogues?* You've got all sorts of thoughts going on in your head, and I've got stuff going on in my head as I write this. I'm writing about internal dialogues, but I am thinking to myself at the same time, *Geez, I hope they enjoy this. I hope nobody falls asleep reading this.*

Your job is to find a way to help your prospect realize that he is going to rent from you. You already know the prospect is going to rent from you. They don't know it yet, so you're going to have to help them realize that. This is a powerful twist for helping you sell to more people.

Part of the challenge at a self-storage facility is that you rarely see your happy customers. You rarely have someone walk in the office and say, "Hey, you guys are doing a good job today. I'll see you later." How many times would that happen to you? But what usually happens is you get the people who complain, so it's easy to become cynical about your customers because you think they're all whiners; they're all spoiled, and they can't be made happy because your thinking is completely twisted by the people you talk to who are the folks having a problem.

The fact of the matter is the flipside. The vast majority of your customers are happy with the convenience and the service you offer. And even though everyone says they hate to be sold to, the fact is that almost everyone enjoys a pleasant sales process. Just help them realize they're going to rent with you and enjoy it.

This is what goes on in your storage prospect's head. They suffer from the *is it syndrome*, and you may suffer from this when you're shopping for things too.

Is it going to be right for me? Is it going to be too expensive? Is it going to last? Is it going to be a hassle if the thing breaks? You have all of these *is it* thoughts going through your head before you make a buying decision, and so does your customer.

Typically, the customer worries if you're going to charge more than it's worth. Is it going to be too expensive? Is it going to be a hassle? Is the place going to be clean? Is it going to be safe?

The customer wants to know if she's in her unit at night that she's going to walk out of there in one piece. She also wants to know if you're going to be a pain to deal with.

Do you think most customer service and most retail salespeople are a pleasure to work with? If you are like most people, you think most sales and customer service people are uninterested, unprofessional, and annoying. Your customers feel the same way. When they walk into your place of business, they expect that your people are going to be less than friendly, less than helpful, less than happy to be at work, less than concerned about their customers' situations, and a pain in the neck to deal with. They're already coming in the door with a chip on their shoulder.

Do you secret shop your competition on a regular basis in person or by phone? If you don't, you should try it; it's enlightening. If you do shop them, how many of your competitors are on the ball, friendly, helpful, do-anything-for-you kind of people? If you find any like that, you'd better hire them right away! Most of your competitors let people answer the phones who have no telephone skills and allow people to manage their operations who have little or no customer service ethic and usually even fewer sales skills. Most of your customers, if you're not the first place they've called or the first place they've come to, already expect you to be gruff, unhelpful, and annoyed that you're being interrupted by a shopper's inquiry.

So this is what you're up against. The people come in with a chip on their shoulder, and you're going to have to do something to knock off that chip. Because they have this chip and assume self-storage people are jerks, they don't want to tell you what their real concerns are. They're afraid that if they open up to you, you're going to take advantage of them, rip them off, give them a crappy storage unit for way too much money, or use the information against them. So rather than tell you their concerns, they're often going to tell you all kinds of other stuff.

You will have people call you up or walk in and say, "I've never stored before. What am I supposed to do?" Those people are easy to talk to because they're open to learning and open to suggestion, but most people don't approach you like that. Most people will say, "How much is one of those" while keeping the chip firmly pressed to their shoulders.

They act that way because they are worried. They are worried about spending too much money because worrying about spending too much money is a respectable and accepted worry. These are the things they'll tell you to express that worry, right? "Too much money," "I have to talk to my spouse," "I'm not ready to do anything," "I have to shop around," "I'm just checking prices." So that's what they tell you, but is that what they're thinking? No.

What they're thinking is they'd really rather hit themselves on the thumb with a hammer than to have to find a storage unit. They're now in a situation that's not happy; it's interrupting their day. In fact, their whole life is interrupted, and they've got all kinds of things they'd rather be doing. They don't want to spend any more money than they have to. They don't trust you because most of the retail people and customer service people they typically deal with are rude at best, and they're wishing they had another option. So how do you overcome that?

You have to be the one who overcomes these preconceived notions of you and your storage place. It is up to you and your frontline people because the prospects are judging you the whole time they're talking to you and you're talking to them. Don't you do this when you're in a restaurant? From the moment a server walks up to you and says, "Hi, I'm so-and-so. I'll be taking care of you tonight," aren't you already keeping score to decide how quick and responsive they are? Are they taking care of your water glass? How much are you going to tip them? Is this going to be a 10 percent? 20 percent?

I have an example. I had lunch one time at a trade show with some folks who I see at a lot of the trade shows, and we had an enjoyable chat about all kinds of stuff, but we had one of those disaster-service lunches. The kitchen didn't get Peggy and Jack's food right. It took the staff four times to get the right plate out to me. And we weren't the only table the restaurant had trouble with. Other tables were getting re-served. It was a small disaster in the grand scheme of things. It wasn't that big of a deal, though. I got my lunch and good conversation; the food was actually good, so I was happy. The interesting thing about the whole situation was the frustration of our waitress. She even sent somebody else to take care of our table because she couldn't handle it anymore.

The folks I was sitting with, Peggy and Jack, said they were at a restaurant a week earlier at home, and it was a disaster too. It was not only a disaster for getting food on time and getting the order right, but the food, too, was terrible. Their waiter did everything he could to make it right, and they were so pleased with how the waiter handled things that he ended up with a good tip.

This is what people are looking for when they deal with you too. They want you to make their experience a good one. You don't have to try terribly hard; you just have to try. They don't really care if your facility is first-generation, second-generation, A-, B-, or C-class. They don't know the difference; they don't care. They just notice how you treat them.

PhoneSmart surveyed self-storage managers about the behavior of people who come into the office to pay their rent by check. We asked: "If your customers—your renters—had to write a check for their rent today, how many of them would know who to write the check out to?" We discovered that when they came and stood at the desk to write a check to the storage company, they had to look to see whom to make the check out to because, in the customer's mind, who do self-storage customers store with? They store with the manager. They usually know the manager's first name. They often don't even know the name of the company.

This is an indicator of what people are comfortable with and want. They want to know who they are dealing with. They want to know that person will make things right. If people feel that way, then it doesn't matter what the name of the company is or what promises or advertisements the company makes.

So while a new customer is talking to you, from the moment you say, "Hello," she is saying to herself, "Is this guy going to be a jerk? Am I going to like this guy? Is he honest? Is he ripping me off?"

People aren't stupid. They can take one look at a storage facility and do the math. They can figure your building costs are way less than other kinds of construction. They can figure you get killed by real estate taxes. They can figure your payroll is next to nothing as a percentage of revenue. They can quickly count up how many units they think you have and multiply that by the rent you are asking them to pay and say to themselves, "Oh, my gosh! This place breaks even at 43 percent occupancy. Oh, geez! It is a gold mine for the owner, and I'm going to get screwed." Most people know what they're looking at.

So when they talk to you as the person running your fictitious storage business, and they say they're concerned about price, what they really want to know is if the person behind the desk thinks it's a good price. If they feel as if the person behind the desk thinks you charge too much, then you're sunk. That's why your people in any business have to assume the close; they have to be comfortable with what you charge; they have to believe that you offer a good value for the money. If that's the impression people get, then your customers accept the price for what it is. When your staff is confident about the pricing, customers accept that your people know what they're talking about, are honest, and have confidence in their offering.

If your people expect that everyone they talk to will have sticker shock, then your staff will hesitantly give the price and quickly duck for cover, so they aren't hurt when the prospect yells, "It costs how much?!"

The prospect thinks that if your staff are squirming, it's because they think your units are too expensive and a lousy deal. This reinforces any initial impression in your prospect's mind that price is a determining factor in choosing storage. It also makes your people price-shy and causes them to tell you that the reason rentals are off-pace this month is because the units are priced too high.

If instead your staff are calm and confident about pricing and focus on the value of your offers and the convenience of doing business with you, your prospects will accept the price for what it is and will see the issue as a matter of value and not a matter of price. Everybody wants to do business with somebody who can instill confidence in a purchase like that.

Feeling confident in a long-term relationship is also important to your prospects. They want to know if you're going to be a jerk if they have a problem because everyone expects there to be a problem with someone they do business with at some point or another. And really, if you have a problem with a company, do you get annoyed about it if the company addresses the problem and takes care of you? You typically say to yourself, "Whatever. I had a problem; they took care of me. Fine."

Customers do not mind having a problem with your company as long as there is a reasonable resolution, and the people they deal with in your company are professional about it and do not act like jerks.

That is why prospects will often ask you a lot of questions up-front, especially about policy issues and processes. They want to know if you have a customer-friendly approach. If they perceive your staff as being great, you win the new customer's business and loyalty. If they perceive your staff as being lousy, you lose the customer's confidence. Perhaps you lose the customer altogether.

There is a saying in the self-storage business (and there may be a similar saying in your industry). It goes like this: *A great facility manager can make a lousy property good, and a lousy facility manager will make a great property lousy.*

A great manager understands the internal dialogue your customers experience and can correctly address those concerns. If you were in the storage business for real, you'd go out from time to time to shop your storage competitors. You would probably find someone who has a property that hasn't been painted for twenty years, is full, and only 2 percent off of the highest market rates. You do the math in your head and figure the place is running at 110 percent economic occupancy. You're thinking, *How is this possible?* You talk to the manager and find out: *Okay, I know how it's possible: the people running this place are friendly, knowledgeable, capable, and helpful. I'm screwed! They have the right manager.*

Then you go down the street to a newer facility and find a beautiful, well-situated store that has been having trouble breaking 60 percent occupancy for three years and is priced the same as the full old dump you just visited. Then you go inside and find out why.

I had this experience at one of the major player's stores. I like to do personal shopping because I can pick up a lot of interesting impressions. I walked in to this particular store and said, "I think I need to get a storage unit today." The store manager had her back turned to me and was reading a paperback book. She turned around and said, "You have to call the phone number on the wall there. They can offer you the special. I can't." She turned back around and went back to her book. I said, "Ah, excuse me. I need to get in today. Can't I just do this with you?" She said, "No, you have to call the number up there. I'm getting ready to go to lunch anyway," and turned back around again. I said to myself, "Wow! This is great. I wish I had a place across the street from them. This is wonderful." Do you think people care about marginal price differences when they can get such a very different customer experience? Do you think they care that much about features, amenities, or updates when they are really looking for someone who can offer a decent experience?

The problem is, of course, that this lousy experience is what people often expect from you and then come to you with a chip on their shoulder. If you understand this and have a good experience waiting for people, they become your customers. It does not have to be a great experience. It just has to be good.

Why do people really decide to rent or not to rent? In every study I've seen, location is the number one reason why people pick a place to store their stuff. So right away if somebody tells you they like your location, it means they have tolerance for features, and they have tolerance for price. They will have tolerance for all kinds of things if they really like your location.

Renters like to have perceived security. You don't have to have armed guards in the place; they just have to look at your place and say to themselves, "Yeah, it looks like the place is pretty secure."

They just need to feel like you've taken enough security precautions, so it's likely going to be secure. Fortunately, the reality is that thefts in a storage facility are rare, but the security precautions must be effective nonetheless.

The appearance of your place also has to be nice. You don't have to have Renoirs on the wall and have professional landscapers come in every other day, but the place has to be comparatively clean and neat. Even if the customers keep their own unit messy, they want at least the rest of the place to look clean and neat. And they want amenities for their money. They want value for their dollar.

Let me ask you this: Do you drive a Kia? If not, why? It's effective transportation. It's got a 100,000-mile warranty. It's well-designed. Why don't more people drive Kias? People want more for their automobile money than just basic transportation. They want something else for their money, so they drive more expensive cars. So if you have or don't have the Kia of storage facilities, it doesn't really matter. People are willing to spend a few extra dollars to get a better location, more perceived security, a few more amenities. And what they're really willing to spend money on is the good attitude of your staff. If you have a good attitude, people don't care if it costs a few bucks more to store with you. They're happy to do it because they know if they have a problem, you'll take care of them.

People would rather spend their money where they're treated well. Have you ever walked out of a retail store because you weren't acknowledged when you were standing around twiddling your thumbs waiting for help? I've taken informal surveys on this question and find that usually three-quarters of an audience at one of my speaking engagements will raise their hands. Your customers feel the same way.

Price is usually the third or fourth reason for choosing a storage unit, yet it's often the first thing out of a prospect's mouth. They usually ask, "How much is it?" Nevertheless, it does not mean what you think it means. You likely live in an area of the country where many languages are spoken. Even in my hometown of Columbia, Missouri, a community of maybe 100,000 people, there are something like forty-two languages spoken by children in the public school's English for Nonnative Speakers program. You must assume that the self-storage prospect speaks a foreign language. "How much is a storage unit?" actually translates into: "Please tell me why I should store with you?"

Here's why people *don't* rent a storage space: A lot of people talk to companies about storage, but their needs change. They reconcile with their spouse; they don't get divorced. The job falls through. Their kid actually does get his own apartment and moves out with his stuff. Their needs change, so they no longer need storage. Sometimes people look into storage while they weigh their options when dealing with a project or circumstance. If you do not help them realize that storage is an ideal solution for anyone and everyone and for every situation, they will often decide another course of action. This is why it is so important to assume the sale and close early. You will lose many of your new customers if you let time pass before your follow-up.

Normally, once someone rents a storage unit, 50 percent will stay for eighteen months or more. Don't let them think too hard about it. Get them in a unit. You surely have something similar going on in your business. Get the sale when people are thinking of buying. Don't wait until something else comes up to stop the sale.

Money is also a factor in why they don't choose storage. Some people do not have discretionary income available. Most people are spending more than they bring in as it is. Many people don't know what storage costs. If someone is on a tight budget, and $50 is too much for a person to spend, then $80 is too much to spend. If your competitor is getting $80 for a unit, and you're getting $100 for a unit, and someone thinks storage costs $50, you both lose because the prospect won't store with anybody. So if you want to get around people's price sensitivity, you have to find out what they're budgeting for storage, what they think storage is going to cost them, and then work within their limits.

So price will be a reason why people decide, "Do you know what? I'm just going to put the stuff in the dumpster. I'll have a yard sale. I'll give it to the Salvation Army."

Or maybe your facility was dirty the day they visited you. Maybe you forgot to sweep out the front walkway. Maybe you've been walking by the trash on the curb because you just walk by it every day and don't bother to look. Maybe you had a fight with your kids before you sent them off to school that morning, and you took that bad attitude to work with you. People are perceptive. If they think your attitude is off, they don't think, *Gosh, he might be having a bad day*, they think, *What did I do to annoy him? I'm dealing with somebody else.*

Here's what happens: You're talking to a current customer at the desk. Someone else walks in. It took you four seconds to make eye contact with the new person instead of two. That's over their tolerance limit; that person is out of there and on to the next storage place. People can think you had a bad attitude, even though you were trying to be helpful. People are quick to judge attitude, so you have to be aware of that and be prepared to meet or exceed a person's desire for a good experience.

Here's what happens when you've done well with your customers: Their internal dialogue goes, "Hmm, well, I don't really want to spend $100, but I guess if that's what it costs, that's okay. She's pretty nice. It looks like a pretty clean place. I've got other things to do; I can't spend all day on this. I might as well just get this done. Okay, fine. I'll take it."

If you can help that person's internal dialogue go, "Seem like nice people. Seems like a nice enough place. Seems like the money's not too bad. Okay, I'll do this," then you're in like Flynn, and the next thing they ask you will be, "How do you want me to pay you?"

How many times have you had this happen when you're dealing with a prospect? The person turns to you to say, "Do you take cash, check, or credit card?" This is a great moment in the sales process. You have helped them talk themselves into buying from you.

Usually you do have to ask them to buy from you, or you have to say, "Here is the paperwork; all I need you to do is fill this out." If the potential buyer's internal dialogue is going in your favor, and you remember to ask for the business, you will win . . . and the customers will have their needs met. You both win.

An important statistic you need to understand if you have a storage facility is *length of stay*. It is a driver of cost and revenue assumptions. You need to know a lot about length of stay for making good long-term decisions. You need to know how many people stay a month, how many stay two months, how many stay six months, how many stay twelve months, how many stay twenty-six months, and you need to know that by class of units. You need to know by small, medium, or large; you need to know the difference between homeowners, apartment renters, students, and military. You need to know all of these statistics to run your business well.

If you don't know all of these statistics, start making notes. If the software that runs your business doesn't give you all of this information, you're going to have to find a roundabout way to get it.

How many businesses have a larger ticket than self-storage? The average storage customer might spend $600, $800, or even $1,000 during a stay. Is your average ticket bigger than that in your business?

Lots of businesses have a bigger ticket: automobile dealers, upscale clothing stores, and furniture stores. An emergency room does, too, along with apartment communities and home remodeling, roofing, and siding contractors.

The point is that the effort and expense it takes to turn your corporate culture into a sales and marketing machine will be well worth the investment. If an industry with customers who have a value of $800 in revenue can be successful in a down economy by adopting a sales culture, what could the impact be for you and your business unit?

Self-storage and other businesses have a lot of short-term, small-ticket customers too. There are a whole lot of people who stay just one to three months, but that's okay, too, isn't it? If they're pumping up your occupancy, and you like your rental rates, and you're selling them boxes, locks, and insurance, renting them a truck, and making sure one out of three of them refer a friend to you, aren't the short-termers great for business too?

This is why I have never understood waiters who are rude to their small-ticket guests. My wife and I went to a high-end steak house to spend time together. We decided to split a meal and have conversation. The waiter about came unglued when he took our order. Small-ticket buyers have friends and Twitter accounts, too, you know. Each customer is not just a transaction but a referral source.

I bring this up to point out that there's a tremendous upside in increasing average lengths of stay or repeat transactions. One very real effect of turning your business into a sales and marketing machine is the better experience your current customers will have.

You have to resell your current customers to a certain extent every month. Are you actively reselling the people who moved in or bought from you last month? Are you even thinking that way? Think about this: What would it do to your bottom line if you could increase your average length of stay by just one month or have just one more transaction a month with each of your customers? What would that do to your bottom line? What would that do to your economic occupancy levels? What would that do to your discounting strategies? That's enormous stuff, isn't it, if you added an extra month of income to the yearly value of each of your customers?

Self-storage customers think to themselves every month, *Should I stay or should I go?* Should they pay or should they move out or quit the storage company?

Some of them are thinking, "Should I get a different size unit?" Do you have a strategy in place to upsize or downsize your current customers rather than letting them move out or quit you? I recently switched from a Grande Mocha to a tall chai. The coffee and tea place kept me as a customer, even though I changed my habit.

If you see one of the customers in your fictitious storage place move a bunch of stuff out of his unit, you can ask, "Hey, do you need to get into a smaller unit?" If you see somebody cramming more stuff in his unit, you can ask, "Hey, do you need to get a little bigger space?" That's a powerful customer-service touch. Many of your customers would think you stopped caring about them when they signed the lease and that you'd only pay attention to them if they were late on the rent. The mere fact that you notice them and continue to keep their best interests in mind could easily result in an extra month's rental.

Until your customers see their storage unit as a part of the household, as an extension of the home, they're thinking every month, *Should I stay or should I go?*

Until a business that rents with you sees its storage unit as its back office, garage, or satellite facility, it's thinking the same thing every month: *One more expense I don't really need. Call up the storage people. Cancel the darn thing.*

There are important thresholds people will cross, and you have to be aware of them. The first threshold is the first month; the first time their first full month's rent is due. If you do any kind of specials or discounts, you've moved someone in partly because he got a cheap deal to get his first month. Now the customer's first full month's rent is due, and he goes (groaning), "Ugh, time to bite the bullet." And then the second month, "Ugh, here we go again." And then the third month, "Oh, geez, this is getting expensive! Should I stay or should I go?"

If you can get them past the third month, the fourth and the fifth month don't seem quite that bad. And then the sixth month comes, and they go, "Gosh, I've been here about half a year now, haven't I? Do I really want to be there that long? Should I stay or should I go?" What do people say when they move in about how long they are going to need a unit? Storage owners sometimes ask, "How long are you going to stay with us?" Most people will say only a month or two, or a few months. Yet often half of them are staying over a year. Why is that? It's not because they're stupid. It's not because they forget to move out. They're happy. Or at least they are not unhappy enough about the storage unit to do anything about it. It's become their extra attic, their extra garage. They learn to love having it because they can hide stuff in there that they don't have to clean up or deal with or put away.

You have a similar buyer cycle in your business. Figure it out.

I heard someone say a wonderful thing at one of my seminars. I asked the audience what they thought people were really buying when they rent a storage unit. I usually get similar responses: room, space, peace of mind, security for their belongings. Yes, these are all a part of the purchase. But here's what someone told me that day. It is a simple and elegant response. What are people buying when they rent storage from you? "They're buying time." They are buying time to decide what to do with their stuff. They're buying time because they don't really want to take care of their situation now. That's especially true if they're moving, they've had a death in the family, they've got favorite items they just don't have room for, or they've got four lawnmowers when they really only need two. They're buying time to figure out what to do with their stuff. Isn't that a wonderful way to look at it? And they're obviously buying a lot of time if half of them are staying more than a year. Be aware that these thresholds of decision happen when people typically stop to examine what they're doing to decide to move forward or not.

What are people really buying from you? Get inside their minds to figure it out.

You have to resell them each month because each month you convince them to stay, their resistance lowers. With every time they pay you, their resistance lowers because paying you becomes increasingly routine over time. If this is the seventeenth time they've now seen the automatic deduction on their bank statement or the automatic charge on their credit card, it does not have nearly the impact as the second or fifth time. When it becomes routine, it becomes a part of their monthly experience. When the payment is also associated with feeling good about buying time, the renter stays another month. The storage unit becomes an extension of the person's home and lifestyle.

When you first got a cell phone, did you think, *I'm not carrying that stupid thing. I'll leave it in the car, or I'll put it in my purse and keep it turned off?* Do you now carry your cell phone on your belt or in your pocket or in your hand? You probably have a smartphone glued to your head now. The same thing happens in self-storage. Acceptance, usage, and experience encourage further acceptance and usage over time.

Here's why people would stay with you: It's convenient. It's an easy place to hide stuff, get stuff out of the way, keep organized, deal with your seasonal items, and keep from cluttering up the house. If you're in a business, it is much cheaper to store your files in your storage facility than it is to take up part of somebody's office. Businesses need to buy time, too. They're always moving people around, moving cubicles, moving desks. It buys them time to deal with their excess inventory and furniture. They don't have to decide what to do with things now; they can stick things in the storage unit; they don't have to worry about how the decision will be made or who has to make it.

Another big reason why they stay is because it's a bigger pain to move out than it is to pay, and that's the simple equation. People think about leaving their storage unit and think to themselves, "Nah, it'll be a big pain to move out. I'll just call in a payment."

Or they look at their credit card or bank statement and see the charge to you. They think to themselves, "I've already spent a bunch of money on storage, but you know what? It would be a huge pain to decide what to do with my stuff and even a bigger pain to move out," and they stay another month. This is exactly the thought process and behavior you need to stimulate in your customers.

If, on the other hand, you have made it a pain for them to stay, they might think, *Do you know what? That SOB at the storage place was rude to me the last time I rolled through there. I don't have to take that crap. I'll show him. I'll just move out one night this week and to heck with him.*

If you can't get your billing systems straight, they also might think to themselves, *Those idiots over-locked me again after I paid my bill on time. I'm done with them! I'm moving out.* If you have caused this sort of thinking in your customers, they don't care if it takes them all weekend, and they have to miss the football game they have been waiting three months to watch, they'll pull their stuff right out of there, and you're stuck with an empty unit.

A lot of times they move out just because the situation has worked itself out. The estate has settled. They've figured out what to do with Grandma's antiques. The new house finally got built after all of the weather delays. They were finally able to get the contractor to finish. They have everything all settled, so they no longer need the storage unit.

Or they're cutting back. They look at their bank statement every month and go, "Hmm, I've got lessons to pay for the kids, and they need new shoes again. Honey, we've got to get rid of the storage unit." That happens. However, if you have made your storage experience pleasant enough, they will delay the actual move-out date a month or two.

You don't want a single renter to move out because you had a lousy attitude. You can't let yourself get caught having a bad day when nothing is working right in the office. Your public face can't show that. You have to make sure your customers feel respected and cared about even if they had what you thought was a silly problem. You can't let on that you thought it was a silly problem. If that's what they picked up from how you handled them, they will think to themselves, "I'll fix you," and they move out.

If your systems stink, you will lose customers needlessly. Is your gate broken more than it is working? Do you have trouble with your access system, so every time the customers use their access codes, their code doesn't work? Then a customer thinks, "Ugh! Why am I paying for this? I could just leave this stuff in a box in my garage, and it'll be fine." Or maybe you've now over-locked them three months in a row after they actually have paid their bill. One of the top complaints we get from current customers in our call center is: "I gave you a check three days ago. Take the damn lock off my unit!"

So if your systems stink, fix them, because it's the easiest way to keep customers. No matter what your business, your customers do not like stupid systems.

There are all kinds of ways you can make it easy for people to stay. One of the most popular ones you're probably doing already with companies you do business with: electronic withdrawals from a checking account or automatic charges on credit cards. This is an easy way to make it less of a pain for people to pay.

Be sensitive to what's a pain and what's a pleasure at your facility, because there's always some kind of balance there between your access, how the doors roll, which way the sun is shining in people's faces, the smell of the place, where dust tends to settle, and all kinds of little things that can make a difference. Be aware of those, and find a way to compensate for each pain or eliminate them.

It is hard to tell from customer reactions what is causing them pain at your store because your typical customers do not want to confront you. Yes, you have some who come in to the office and say,

"Look, this is the second time this has happened. If it happens a third time, I'm moving out. So whatever your problem is, fix it!" You've got to love those people because you know if you fix the problem, they'll stay forever. They will feel good that they confronted you, you did what you were supposed to do, and now they're happy. If only all of your customers who were annoyed would do that, your average customer lifetime value would probably double. But that's not what most people do. Have you ever had lousy service at a restaurant and said nothing about it, tipped 15 percent anyway, and just never come back? We have all done that. That's exactly what our customers do too.

If someone says to you, "Gosh, we're moving out. It's been so swell. Thank you," you do not know if they are being sincere unless you ask them questions about their experience. Otherwise you have no way of knowing if they're driving out of your parking lot, thinking, *That SOB; it's the last time he'll see me!*

We all have done that to vendors or suppliers or providers. We say, "Thank you. It's been nice dealing with you," and then we mumble our true feelings under our breath as we walk away.

So be aware that some percentage of people are moving out and quitting you because something happened that was a pain to them, and you're completely unaware of what that pain was. If you'd only known that pain, you would have fixed it. So if you want to know how your customers are answering the question "Should I rent or should I not rent?" you have to listen to them. If they're giving you feedback, you have to ask them a few more questions. You've got to anticipate the concerns that people are going to have because most people have the same concerns I have been writing about. The concerns that new renters have should be posted on the screen in your mind's eye. Don't you get many of the same questions all day long? Yes, sometimes you get some interesting, off-the-wall ones, but it's usually the same questions. You know what people's concerns are, so anticipate those concerns and show people that you have *them* covered. We know what people are looking for. We know what bothers people. We know what they're trying to avoid. We know what they are afraid of. We know what they like. Let your customers know that you know all these things, and they will feel much better about choosing you.

If your customers are not talking to you, then you have to talk to them. You have to find some ways to get them into the office, get them on the phone, or get them by email, because most people are busy. They don't really want to stop to visit with you. They have twenty-seven things on their to-do list, and they still have to-do items left from yesterday to get done. So get them in the door! Send them a coupon, put fresh-baked cookies on the counter, wander around the property when people are out there accessing their units and visit with them. Find out what their concerns are. You may not know half of what their concerns are because you're busy doing what you need to do to run your business. It is difficult to make the time to visit with customers because there is always some fire for you to put out. You have to make the time to go out and talk to people to find out what they're thinking. The very fact that you bothered to ask them will get you another month's stay out of a person. Find out what they're really concerned about because many times people won't tell you their real concern until you've talked to them.

Do you coach and counsel your employees on a regular basis? What's the response when you say, "Hey, how's everything going?" Your employee says, "Fine."

If you don't ask a second question, you won't have a single clue what's going on in their mind. The same thing happens with your customers. When you say, "Hey, how's everything going?" and they say "Fine," you have not gotten any information. You have to ask specific questions. Then you find out that their unit gets flooded with debris every time they have the door open and the wind blows, and it's annoying the heck out of them.

So here's the outcome. If you do at least a few of these things you've read about, fewer people are going to choose not to rent. Fewer people are going to choose to move out. Here's another thing to consider: The cost of doing all of this is what? There is no cost because everything I have written about comes down to your attitudes and perceptions. Those are all free. Anything you do from this book will improve your business and your revenues. It will take a bit of self-examination. You have to catch yourself when you're having a bad attitude. You have to catch yourself when you're not up to par in your customer service. So there is some cost to your pride and your self-esteem from time to time, but what's the potential impact on your bottom line? It's huge. If you increased the conversion rates of the number of people you sell to compared with the number of people you talk to by even five points, what would that do to your business? What would it do if you increased your average customer tenure by only one month or one transaction? You'd be looking at expanding your business because your revenue would be at the top of the market.

Now that you have had a chance to look at a specific industry case study, how will you go about improving the sales culture in your unit or your company?

You have four jobs in front of you if you want to implement the strategies and tactics I have laid out for you:

1. Create a sales culture

2. Learn the basics of sales

3. Apply sales skills to your specific industry

4. Get inside your customer's mind

Each one of these activities will bring you big rewards in building a better business and in pushing profit to your bottom line. Each activity will improve your sales culture.

If the people who run self-storage businesses could make a major cultural shift from running a basic property management business to running sales and marketing operations with significant ecommerce components, couldn't your business unit or your company take these four steps and dramatically change the course of its history?

If you could picture yourself creating and implementing great sales culture innovations at your fictitious storage business during the last few sections of this book, why can't you take this exercise and put it into practice in your real workplace?

What is stopping you from applying this lesson to your situation? Are you afraid you won't get buy-in from your superiors? Don't be. They don't even have to know what you are doing until you are able to show successes to them. Are you afraid you won't get buy-in from your coworkers? Don't be. They don't need to know what you are doing until you can show them big successes. Are you afraid the people reporting to you won't jump in to help you make it happen? Okay. You should be a little afraid of that. But remember the steps of resistance and acceptance people go through when working through cultural or operational changes. Lead them through.

Every step of the way, you'll be able to show your team how little shifts in sales phraseology, little shifts in behavior, and little shifts in their own thought processes will bring positive reactions and results. You don't have to make a disruptive noise with this. Just start using the language of selling and start acting like you have a better sales culture, and the cultural shift will begin to gain momentum.

If an industry as dull as renting storage units to people can become a sales and marketing culture that saved an entire generation from having to start out their adult lives with nothing, you can get a 10 percent improvement in revenue. If a whole industry that never had to think about selling for a second can become driven by conversion rates and customer referral incentives, you can get your team members' internal dialogues using the language of sales.

A company that has .0027 market share of the entire storage realm of North America set out to master the first rule of selling and in turn to create a sales culture. This was a reaction to changing times and a hedge against a coming economic storm. StorageMart succeeded because its people simplified this seemingly gargantuan task into the four steps you have been reading about and worked diligently to make it all happen. Not only did this approach bring solid results to StorageMart, it also inspired an entire industry to transform itself into what consumers would want to support and participate in. You should take some inspiration from this story, too.

Your sales culture could be a lot better. If you get started as soon as you close this book, your sales culture will be a lot better soon. Start by passing this book to a coworker or friend. Good luck—and good selling!

About Tron Jordheim

T ron Jordheim is one of those entrepreneurs who are always making something out of nothing. He started his first business in the sixth grade with a roll of paper towels and a can of window cleaner. He has been at it ever since. He took his interest in protection dog training and created a whole new business model that put him through college. Tron helped New York City start its police K-9 unit. He ran man-dog security patrols for Pan Am airlines at JFK airport and was the team captain for the United States team that competed at the European Championship for German Shepherd Dog Clubs in 1982. He was sought after as a seminar leader and training advisor for competition dog clubs across the country. When the flip-flop in international exchange rates took the profit out of his business of importing German shepherds from Germany and Austria, Tron went to work as a cold-call salesperson for the Great Bear Bottled Water Company in New York City. They gave him the Upper West Side of Manhattan, which was the worst-performing territory in New York. It wasn't long before it was one of the best-performing territories, and he was being sent out to work in other markets as a trainer and sales-blitz leader. Great Bear was eventually taken over by the Perrier Group and its Poland Spring Water division, which made known its intent to eliminate the sales force and fire all the Great Bear middle-management people. That's when Tron moved to central Missouri where the commute is short and the prairie wind is bitter. Once in Missouri, Tron went to work to help grow a Culligan Bottled Water franchise from 1,200 customers to 6,800. It became the Culligan Bottled Water franchise with the highest per capita penetration of bottled water accounts of any in the nine-hundred-plus dealers in the Culligan network. It wasn't long before Tron became a verb. After training and consulting for other bottled water companies and other Culligan dealers, salespeople stopped going selling and started going "Troning" to get more customers. His booklet, *Setting Coolers*, and his work in the field are two of the reasons many people you know use water five gallons at a time. After Coke and Pepsi decided to get into the bottled water business in a big way, Tron decided to look for other opportunities. As it turned out, the massive distribution network of Coke and Pepsi and the convenience of small bottles of water did cause the five-gallon water business to plateau dramatically. And then along came an opportunity to grow the PhoneSmart business from the drawing board. Tron not only grew the rollover sales support end of the business but also launched a successful secret shopping/quality assurance business unit and an Internet-led distribution unit. When PhoneSmart's parent company, StorageMart, saw that it needed to become a master of self-storage marketing, Tron was selected to lead the way. Tron continues to be sought after as a public speaker, sales trainer, and consultant. His success as a speaker and trainer was affirmed when he was accepted as a member of the National Speakers Association. Tron has worked as a speaker, trainer, and consultant with businesses and trade associations in the United States, Canada, United Kingdom, Mexico, and Spain. His sessions on sales, marketing, people management, and business development are worth the travel.

CPSIA information can be obtained at www.ICGtesting.com
Printed in the USA
BVOW08s1151161013

333882BV00003B/387/P